W9-AWG-539

12/25/14

A Gift for

MAXWELL

Presented by

PA PA & MARY

I Wish
I Knew That
U.S. Presidents

I Wish
I Knew That
U.S. Presidents

Cool Stuff You
Need to Know

Edited by Patricia A. Halbert

**Reader's
Digest**

The Reader's Digest Association, Inc.
New York, NY / Montreal

PROJECT STAFF

Project Editor: Patricia A. Halbert

Contributing Writer: Susan Randol

Designer: Rich Kershner

Illustrator: Andrew Pinder

READER'S DIGEST TRADE PUBLISHING

Senior Art Director: George McKeon

Editorial Director, Trade Publishing: Neil Wertheimer

Manufacturing Manager: Elizabeth Dinda

Associate Publisher, Trade Publishing: Rosanne McManus

President and Publisher, Trade Publishing: Harold Clarke

Library of Congress Cataloging in Publication Data

I wish I knew that : U.S. presidents : cool stuff you need to know / edited by Patricia A. Halbert.
   p. cm.
  Includes index.
  ISBN 978-1-60652-360-5
  1. Presidents--United States--Biography--Miscellanea--Juvenile literature. 2. Presidents--United
States--History--Miscellanea--Juvenile literature. I. Halbert, Patricia A.
  E176.1.I138 2012
  973.09'9--dc23
  [B]

                                   2011039347

Reader's Digest is committed to both the quality of our products and the service we provide
to our customers. We value your comments, so please feel free to contact us:

   The Reader's Digest Association, Inc.

   Adult Trade Publishing

   44 S. Broadway

   White Plains, NY 10601

For more Reader's Digest products and information, visit our website:

   www.rd.com (in the United States)

   www.readersdigest.ca (in Canada)

Printed in the United States of America

3 5 7 9 10 8 6 4 2

"The presidency has made every man
who occupied it, no matter how small,
bigger than he was; and no matter how big,
not big enough for its demands."

LYNDON B. JOHNSON
36th President of the United States

CONTENTS

INTRODUCTION

"I do solemnly swear that I will faithfully execute the Office of the President of the United States, and will to the best of my Ability, preserve, protect and defend the Constitution of the United States."

With these simple words, every four years, one person takes on the hardest job in the world—president of the United States of America.

What are the duties of the president? Enforce every federal law of the land. Approve or reject every new law Congress makes. Meet with the leaders of other nations and find ways to get along. Run the largest and most powerful military in history and, if necessary, lead it to war.

To do the job right, you need extraordinary skill at striking deals and making agreements between people who rarely agree on anything. It also helps to be an excellent speaker, not only to inspire the nation and show it the way, but also to get it to follow. One other part of the job: When anything goes wrong, you usually get the blame.

What are the job qualifications? On paper, not much. You must be a natural-born U.S. citizen, at least 35 years old, and must have lived in the United States for at least 14 years. Other than that, anyone is eligible.

The president of the United States has tremendous power, but that power is not unlimited. The last thing our Founding Fathers wanted was a king. The president, for example, can serve only two terms and cannot make new laws. Making

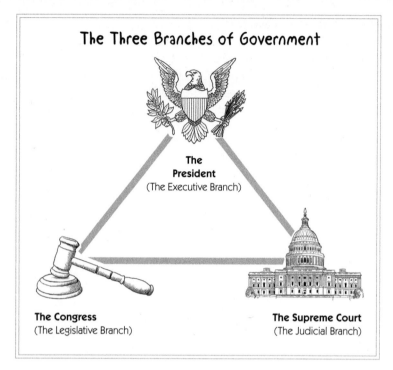

The Three Branches of Government

**The
President**
(The Executive Branch)

The Congress
(The Legislative Branch)

The Supreme Court
(The Judicial Branch)

new laws is Congress's job. And the president cannot decide what a particular law is trying to say—that is the job of the Supreme Court.

Picture a triangle. In the three corners you have president, Congress, and the Supreme Court keeping an eye on each other, neither one letting another get too powerful. This is called a system of checks and balances, and it is tug-of-war, arm wrestling, chess, poker, and a staring contest all rolled into one.

No one said being CEO of the USA was easy. As President Eisenhower put it: "No easy problems ever come to the president of the United States. If they are easy to solve, somebody else has solved them."

Forty-three men have taken on the challenge. Of those forty-three, nine (including some of the greatest) never went to college; nearly half had never worked in Washington, D.C. before; nine were born poor in log cabins; others were from very rich families; eight were born subjects of the English king; four were assassinated in office; six were attacked and almost killed; and four died on the job of natural causes.

One was never married; one was married in the White House; one had fifteen children and one had only an adopted son. The tallest was six-foot-four, the shortest was five-foot-four. The oldest was 69, the youngest was 42.

All had great hopes. Some did brilliant jobs, some were just so-so. Several were good, and a few—through bumbling, cheating, or overstepping their authority—were downright bad. Two—almost three—were put on trial by the Senate. But a few have been truly great leaders, making our nation bigger, stronger, saving not only the United States, but also the world.

"The presidency has made every man who occupied it, no matter how small, bigger than he was," said President Lyndon Johnson, "and no matter how big, not big enough for its demands."

Every president, in his day, was a bigger-than-life celebrity. The whole world was watching. Not because of his glamour or power, but because he had been put at the controls of one of the greatest experiments in history—the experiment to see if people really can get along without kings and emperors and dictators telling them what to do, and if people really can rule themselves with freedom and justice for everyone—the experiment called the United States.

Forty-three men have passed that unfolding experiment on to us. Let's meet them.

MEET THE
PRESIDENTS

GEORGE WASHINGTON
Father of Our Country

"I can foresee that nothing but the rooting out of slavery can perpetuate the existence of our union."

Born
February 22, 1732
Pope's Creek, Virginia

Political Party
Federalist

Vice President
John Adams

First Lady
Martha

Stepchildren
John "Jacky," and Martha "Patsy"

Pets
Vulcan, Madame Moose, Sweet Lips, and Searcher, all hounds

King of America

When General George Washington's army defeated the British in the Revolutionary War, some of the officers began talking about the possibility of making Washington king of their new country of America. Washington hated the idea.

When he was elected first president of the United States of America, he won all of the electoral votes. (He is the only president who has ever been elected unanimously.) When it came time to swear him into office, he had to borrow $100 from a friend (he spent all his money on the war and hadn't been paid back yet) to travel from Mount Vernon, his home in northern Virginia, to attend his inauguration ceremony in New York City. He was a few days late—56 to be exact.

Our First President

Washington helped create a new type of democratic government when he led the Constitutional Convention in 1787, including the idea that the federal government would consist of three different branches (the legislative, judicial, and executive). Later, as the leader of the executive branch, President Washington created the first "cabinet," or group of advisers. He insisted on staying out of a war between France and England, in order to give the U.S. time to grow stronger, even though two of his most important advisers did not agree with him. He also helped select the new capital of the nation, named Washington in his honor, and helped plan its design.

A Big Man With Bad Teeth

At six-foot-two, 200 pounds, Washington was a big man. He wore size 13 boots. He had reddish-blond hair, and his face was scarred from smallpox he got on a trip to Barbados when he was a teenager—the only foreign country he ever visited. He also had terrible problems with his teeth. When he took the oath as president, in fact, he had only one tooth left and continually experimented with different kinds of false teeth made from ivory, hippo teeth, lead, and even some of his old teeth recycled. He owned six white horses and had their teeth brushed every morning. (Can you imagine why?)

When Washington was a boy, he grew up on a farm in Virginia. He hiked seven miles to school and back until he was 12 years old. He loved the outdoors, particularly fishing and foxhunting. As a young man, he worked as a surveyor,

FUN FACT

George Washington is the only president who did not live in the White House—because it hadn't been built. In fact, the capital of the United States was located in New York and then in Philadelphia during Washington's two terms as president.

hiking across all kinds of rugged landscapes measuring out large pieces of land. He carried a portable sundial, a kind of pocket watch.

Washington loved ice cream and in the summer of 1790, our first president ate his way through $200 worth of ice cream made in New York and brought to his home in Mount Vernon. In the days before ice cream makers were invented, it took a long time to make ice cream by hand. After a visit to Philadelphia, Washington brought back a machine that could turn cream into ice. He soon added metal ice cream pots to his kitchen so he could have his favorite treat whenever he wanted.

Washington never had any children of his own, but his wife, Martha, had two young children—Jacky and Patsy—from her first marriage and he raised them as his own.

Remembering George Washington

Seventeen cities, thirty-one counties, one state, and our nation's capital are named after Washington. He is considered one of our greatest presidents because he saw our nation through one of its most difficult times—its birth.

ON THE MONEY

The Treasury Department can't say why certain presidents and statesmen were chosen for different kinds of money. However, the secretary of the treasury usually picks the design, unless a design is chosen by Congress. The secretary makes the final decision, with help from the Bureau of Engraving and Printing (BEP), which prints the new money. The Commission on Fine Arts takes a last look before the design is ready to go.

Here is a list of presidents whose portraits are on different values of paper money and the year when they first appeared:

$1 George Washington, 1869
$2 Thomas Jefferson, 1869
$5 Abraham Lincoln, 1914
$20 Andrew Jackson, 1928
$50 Ulysses S. Grant, 1929
$500 William McKinley, 1928
$1,000 Grover Cleveland, 1928
$5,000 James Madison, 1918
$100,000 Woodrow Wilson, 1934

Can anyone's picture appear on money?

By law, only portraits of deceased persons can appear on our currency, and they must be persons whose places in history the American people know well. For example, two famous Americans who weren't presidents but appear on money are Alexander Hamilton on the $10 and Benjamin Franklin on the $100.

FUN FACT

The only woman's portrait to be on the front of paper money was First Lady Martha Washington on the $1 silver certificate in 1886 and 1891.

∽ **FAMOUS FIRST LADIES** ∽

First ladies are not elected to their position, but they play an important role in how Americans—and the world—view the president. Some became beloved White House hostesses while others (generally in more recent times) adopted social and political causes of their own. Some were unhappy losing their privacy, while others loved being in the spotlight. Here is the first of eight first ladies who made unique contributions to the presidency and to America.

MARTHA WASHINGTON

June 2, 1731–May 22, 1802

Born in Virginia

The nation's first First Lady, Martha Washington grew up on a plantation near Williamsburg, Virginia, with three brothers and five sisters. Like most young women of her day, Martha received little schooling. But she had a quick mind that soaked up information and questioned what went on around her.

Two Marriages

When she was 18 years old, Martha married Daniel Parke Custis, a wealthy planter who was 20 years older than she was. They had four children, but two of them died. Then

Daniel died, too. Two years later, Martha met Colonel George Washington. They were married, and although the couple did not have children together, George raised her son and daughter as his own.

President Washington

When the Revolutionary War began in 1775, George became commander-in-chief of the Continental Army. Although Martha wanted her husband to stay at Mount Vernon, she knew that the country needed him, too. When the war was over, there was no election campaign but George was unanimously named president.

Loved by Soldiers

Martha did not like being First Lady, but she saw it as her duty and did it well. She held dinners and invited the public to visit, although some citizens felt these gatherings were too fancy. She was loved by the Revolutionary War veterans because she often helped them when they were in need.

Home Again

Martha was happy to return to her home in Mount Vernon when her husband's time as president was over. She told a friend, "The General and I feel like children just released from school." George lived to spend only another two years with Martha. When she died three years after him, Martha was buried beside her beloved George at Mount Vernon.

FUN FACT

Martha Washington was the first presidential widow to receive free postage from Congress because she had to buy so many stamps to mail replies to the letters people sent her when her husband died.

JOHN ADAMS

Atlas of Independence

"I must study politics and war that my sons may have liberty to study mathematics and philosophy."

Born
October 30, 1735
Braintree
(now Quincy),
Massachusetts

Political Party
Federalist

Vice President
Thomas Jefferson

First Lady
Abigail

Children
Abigail, John Quincy,
Susanna, Charles,
and Thomas

Pets
Cleopatra, a horse;
Juno and Satan, dogs

A New House for the President

Born and raised outside of Boston, John Adams graduated from Harvard College in 1755. His great-great-grandparents were among the Pilgrims who landed on Plymouth Rock in 1620. When he was elected president, after serving as Washington's vice president, the nation's capital was still in Philadelphia. When the new capital of Washington, D.C., was ready in 1800, President Adams, traveling with his family, got lost in the woods trying to find the White House. Once in his new—but drafty and damp—home, Adams wrote: "May none but honest and wise men ever rule under this roof."

Two Views of the Country

In those days, the candidate getting the second-most votes became vice president. That's how Thomas Jefferson became Adams' vice president. However, the two men did not agree on what the brand-new government should be. Adams wanted the government to grow larger and have a big army, and he wanted to raise taxes to pay for it all. Jefferson thought the government should stay small. By the end of Adams' term in office, he and Jefferson were so angry at each other that when Jefferson beat Adams in the next presidential election, Adams did not go to his swearing-in ceremony. Years later, however, the ice melted and the two Founding Fathers became friends again and wrote many letters to each other, discussing the direction of the country.

The Adams Presidency

Adams kept the United States neutral during the war between France and Britain, giving the U.S. time to build a strong army and navy. But French ships attacked U.S. ships to stop them from trading with Britain. Adams eventually worked out a treaty with France that stopped this undeclared war. He also signed the Alien and Sedition Acts, which some said protected the United States from its enemies, but others said were written to stop people from criticizing the government.

An Important Date

Adams and Jefferson were the only two presidents who signed the Declaration of Independence, which Jefferson wrote. It was dated July 4, 1776. Strangely enough, both John Adams in Boston and Thomas Jefferson in Virginia died within hours of each other on the same day, July 4, 1826—the 50th anniversary of the Declaration of Independence.

FUN FACTS

John Adams' last words before he died were, "Thomas Jefferson survives." He didn't know that Jefferson had died a few hours earlier.

★★★

John Adams didn't like his job as vice president under George Washington. He was frustrated and bored by this job—which he called "the most insignificant office."

A HOME FOR OUR PRESIDENTS

How the White House Came to Be

When it was time to build a house for the president to live in, George Washington wanted to make it a grand palace. In the spring of 1791, he asked French architect Pierre Charles L'Enfant to create a plan. But when the men in charge of paying for the building saw the plan, they were not happy.

Without waiting for permission to begin, L'Enfant started to work. Secretary of State Thomas Jefferson finally fired him, but not before the cellars were dug and some of the materials for the building had already been delivered.

Jefferson instead decided to hold a contest to design plans for the president's house and for the Capitol building where Congress would be doing business. The winner of the contest was James Hoban, an Irish architect who received a prize of $500. His plan was for an elegant mansion, and Washington and the commissioners thought it would be just perfect—and cost much less money.

In October 1792, the cornerstone was laid. But in order for the Congress to have a place to do its work, it was decided that the Capitol and other government buildings be built first, so work on the president's house was delayed.

Abigail Adams's Big, Fancy (But Empty) Laundry Room

When the new home, which became known as the White House, was finally completed, the first president to move in was John Adams with his wife, Abigail, in November 1800. Abigail called it "a castle of a House," "built for ages to come." The problem was that the house wasn't even finished. Only half of the rooms were completed. There wasn't even enough furniture for the family. The lawn was full of tree stumps, weeds, and piles of rubble, and there was even an outdoor toilet where everyone could see it!

"Not one room or chamber is finished," the First Lady complained. She didn't have enough help to keep all the fireplaces burning to heat the house. There were no fences to make a yard so the family could sit outdoors. And the elegant East Room, which was supposed to be for the president to use for entertaining guests, wasn't ready so Abigail used it as place to hang and dry her laundry.

Lucky for Mrs. Adams, she didn't have to live in the White House for long. John Adams lost the presidency to Thomas Jefferson, and by March, Abigail was back home in Massachusetts. Jefferson, who had designed his own house in Virginia, quickly set to work on finishing the president's house, changing it inside and out.

THOMAS JEFFERSON

The Sage of Monticello

"Every generation needs a new revolution."

Born
April 13, 1743
Shadwell, Virginia

Political Party
Democratic-
Republican

Vice Presidents
Aaron Burr
George Clinton

First Lady
Martha

Children
Martha, Mary, and
four children who
died in infancy

Pets
Mockingbird, dogs,
horses, and bears

Man of the People

After he was sworn in as president in 1801, Thomas Jefferson walked across the street to a boardinghouse to get some dinner. There were no empty seats, so he waited. When he moved into the White House, he stopped one custom that General Washington had started—the president bowing to visitors. Jefferson shook hands instead.

Jefferson did not like stuffiness or fancy clothes. His idea of an enjoyable evening was to have people over to talk about books and ideas. He had a round table made so that everyone sitting at it would feel equal. Sometimes he would wear his slippers to dinner. He hated appearing in public, but once ate a tomato in front of people to prove that the strange, new vegetable was not poisonous.

One of his greatest loves was books. His collection of 6,000 volumes became the first Library of Congress. In the White House, Jefferson had a pet mockingbird named Dick that rode on his shoulder and hopped up the stairs next to him when he went up to bed. Jefferson rode his horse for at least two hours nearly every day.

Expanding to the West

In 1803, Jefferson bought 828,000 square miles of land from France. Known as the Louisiana Purchase, this acquisition doubled the size of our country, for a mere $15 million. Then he sent his Virginia neighbor's son, Meriwether Lewis, and Captain William Clark to explore the area and try to find a boat route to the Pacific Ocean. When they returned from what is now called the Lewis and Clark Expedition, they brought Jefferson some huge bears they had captured. Jefferson had them displayed in cages on the White House lawn for everyone to see.

Inventor, Musician, Architect

Jefferson liked to invent things. The swivel chair, a letter-copying machine, and the dumbwaiter were just some of his ideas. He played the violin, spoke six languages, and taught himself architecture. He designed and built his home, Monticello, and the nearby University of Virginia.

Thinking Ahead

Like his fellow Virginia farmer George Washington, Jefferson owned slaves. And like him, Jefferson realized that the evil of slavery would be one of the biggest problems the nation, as a free people, would have to solve. In 1808 Jefferson banned the import of slaves from Africa.

FUN FACTS

Thomas Jefferson came up with an early version of the wooden coat hanger.

★★★

Jefferson wrote the epitaph for his own gravestone. It does not mention the fact that he was president of the United States.

MAN OF MANY TALENTS

Thomas Jefferson Started the World's Biggest Library

Among America's great statesmen, Thomas Jefferson stands out as a man who was interested in an amazing number of things. He was always busy doing and learning. He designed and watched over every detail of the building of his home at Monticello. He managed the farm and all its workers. He was interested in law, geography, plants, natural history, music, and fine food and wine. He wanted to know about everything, and he wrote about anything that interested him. His writings on agriculture alone fill a 704-page book. He loved to read and his personal library was used to start the Library of Congress in 1815.

When the government moved to Washington, D.C. in 1800, Congress decided to start a library. The first shipment of books came from London, packed in 11 trunks. During the War of 1812, British soldiers came to Washington and burned the Capitol building, and all the books from London were destroyed. Thomas Jefferson offered to sell the government his personal library of 6,487 volumes. Many congressmen jumped at the chance; others weren't so sure. The collection, after all, contained books in foreign languages and story books, which the members of Congress felt weren't serious subjects for a government library. Jefferson's offer was finally accepted, but at first, the library was only for the use of the Congress. When Thomas Jefferson became president, the president's office could use it, and by the 1850s, the public was also welcome.

The collection now fills 535 miles of shelves in three enormous buildings. Among its treasures are rare texts: the oldest surviving book printed in the U.S., documents of the first 14 congresses, early Hawaiian books, a scientific paper written by Copernicus, Oriental scrolls, and medieval manuscripts. The most valuable book is a 1455 Gutenberg Bible, the first book ever printed with movable type. And it has books written in 470 languages.

Only about one-fourth of the items in the library are books. There are also four million maps that fill two acres of cabinets. There are nine million photographs of the Old West, the Civil War, and such important events as the Wright Brothers' first airplane flight. There are papers written by America's greatest inventors like Robert Fulton, Thomas Edison, and Alexander Graham Bell. More films, government papers, and music are stored here than anywhere else on earth. And 10,000 items are added every day!

Today, the collections of the world's greatest library don't just sit on the shelves. Thanks to Thomas Jefferson, they can be studied and enjoyed by everyone.

JAMES MADISON

Father of the Constitution

"If men were angels, no government would be necessary."

Born
March 16, 1751
Port Conway, Virginia

Political Party
Democratic-Republican

Vice Presidents
George Clinton
Elbridge Gerry

First Lady
Dolley

Pet
A green parrot belonging to Mrs. Madison

The Bill of Rights

One of only two presidents (along with Washington) who signed the U.S. Constitution—the set of rules and laws for governing the country—James Madison never thought the Constitution went far enough to protect individual rights. So before he became president, he pushed Congress to pass the Bill of Rights (the first ten amendments), which spells out and guarantees things like freedom of speech, freedom of religion, and the right to a trial by jury if someone's accused of a crime.

The War of 1812

Even though the British had surrendered in the American Revolution, they hadn't really given up. On the high seas, they kept stealing U.S. ships and cargo, and even kidnapped American sailors and forced them to serve in the British navy. On the frontier, the British were giving weapons to the Indians so they could attack American settlers.

By 1812, the United States had had enough and President Madison declared war on England, a kind of second war of independence. At first, the War of

1812 didn't go well. The U.S. wasn't ready. The British invaded Washington and burned the Capitol building and the White House. President Madison wasn't home at the time, but luckily his wife Dolley was. When she heard the British were coming, she calmly packed up all of her husband's important papers and a famous painting of George Washington and got away safely.

"The Star-Spangled Banner" is a poem about the British bombarding Fort McHenry in Baltimore during the War of 1812, which the U.S. eventually won.

Personal Notes

At five-foot-four and 100 pounds, Madison was the smallest of all the presidents. He was the first president to stop wearing knickers and start wearing long pants. He graduated from the College of New Jersey, which eventually became Princeton. He had a scar on his nose and used to joke that he got it defending his country—actually, it was from frostbite he got riding his horse home from a debate on a cold, cold night. After two terms, he retired to his home in Virginia and helped Thomas Jefferson build the University of Virginia and work on ending slavery.

FUN FACT

James Madison was called the "Father of the Constitution" because he worked very hard to create it, but he wanted to give credit to other people who worked on it, too. He said that the Constitution was "the work of many heads and many hands."

DOLLEY MADISON

May 20, 1768–July 12, 1849

Saving a Symbol

A gracious hostess, Dolley Madison is remembered for saving a famous portrait of George Washington—an important American symbol—when the British set fire to the White House during the War of 1812.

Two Marriages

Dolley Payne was born into a family in North Carolina that freed their slaves and moved to Philadelphia. At the age of 21, she married John Todd, who died—along with their infant son—from yellow fever only three years later. Not long after his death, she met James Madison, the congressman from Virginia, who would later become president. They married when she was 26 and he was 43, and they eventually moved to Washington when President Jefferson made Madison his secretary of state.

A Beloved Hostess

Jefferson, a widower, asked Dolley Madison to serve as his hostess at the White House, a job she loved and did gracefully and extremely well. She was able to use her hostess experience when her husband became president, making all visitors feel welcome and important. One of the best-loved presidential wives, she used her warm personality to make the White House the center of Washington's lively social life.

The War of 1812

When the British army marched toward the White House in 1814, about to set it on fire, Dolley Madison refused to leave until a portrait of George Washington was taken down from the wall and sent away to protect it from being destroyed. She packed up important papers, silverware, and other valuable items before fleeing the White House herself.

Retirement

The Madisons left the White House in 1817 and retired to their home in Virginia. When the her husband died in 1836, Dolley Madison moved back to Washington, D.C., where Congress gave her a seat in the House of Representatives (which had never been done for any other American woman). She died at the age of 81 in the nation's capital.

FUN FACT

President Zachary Taylor called Dolley Madison "our first lady for a half-century" at her funeral in 1849. The term "First Lady" stuck and has been popular since Abraham Lincoln was president.

JAMES MONROE
Era of Good Feelings President

"Our country may be likened to a new house. We lack many things but we possess the most precious of all—liberty!"

Born
April 28, 1758
Westmoreland
County, Virginia

Political Party
Democratic-
Republican

Vice President
Daniel D. Tompkins

First Lady
Elizabeth

Children
Eliza, James, and Maria

Pet
A spaniel belonging
to Maria

A Young Patriot

James Monroe's parents died when he was a teenager, and he was in college at William and Mary in Williamsburg, Virginia, when the Revolutionary War started. He was just 17 when he and a bunch of his classmates raided the British armory at the Governor's Mansion down the street and got away with 200 muskets and 300 swords, which they sneaked to the Virginia militia.

Monroe became an officer in Washington's army when he was only 18 and rose to the rank of major. He was with General Washington when he crossed the Delaware and was with him during that dreadful winter at Valley Forge. He was terribly wounded and nearly killed capturing the British cannons at Trenton, New Jersey.

New States: Slave or Free?

After the war, Monroe joined Thomas Jefferson's law practice and studied to become a lawyer. By the time Monroe ran for president, America was enjoying an economic boom. He got every electoral vote except one—and that delegate said he voted against Monroe only so that George Washington would be the only president ever elected unanimously. The good feelings did not last, however. In 1819, the U.S. fell into an economic depression. Then people started arguing about whether Missouri should join the United States as a slave state or as a non-slave state. President Monroe signed a compromise, which said that Missouri would be a slave state and Maine would be a free state. The Missouri Compromise led to even more debates about whether slavery would be allowed in new states and territories.

Monroe pressured Spain into selling Florida to the U.S. In fact, during his two terms, the number of states in the United States increased from 15 to 24.

The Monroe Doctrine

James Monroe is probably best known for the Monroe Doctrine, which told European kings and queens they couldn't start new colonies in the Americas. The Monroe Doctrine was drafted by the secretary of state—and future president—John Quincy Adams.

JOHN QUINCY ADAMS

Old Man Eloquent

"If your actions inspire others to dream more, learn more, do more, and become more, you are a leader."

Born
July 11, 1767
Braintree
(now Quincy),
Massachusetts

Political Parties
Federalist,
Democratic-
Republican, Whig

Vice President
John C. Calhoun

First Lady
Louisa

Children
George Washington,
John, Charles, and
Louisa

Pet
An alligator

World Traveler

When he was eight years old, John Quincy Adams watched the Battle of Bunker Hill from his farm near Boston. At 10 he traveled with his father, John Adams, to Europe and learned to speak French and Dutch. While he was still a teenager, he got a job with the U.S. embassy in Russia. By the time he came home and graduated from Harvard, he figured his career would be in international diplomacy.

Political Career

Adams was an ambassador under President Washington and under his father, John Adams, the second president; a U.S. senator under President Jefferson; an ambassador under President Madison; and secretary of state under President Monroe.

Being president of the United States was his least favorite job. He wanted the government to start building lots of bridges and roads so the United States could grow and prosper, but he couldn't convince Congress to spend the money. Why? He refused to play party politics, making deals and promises and trades for this and that. He stuck instead to his principles and ended up making lots of enemies.

A Presidential Swimmer

Adams used to get up at five o'clock every morning, start a fire, read his Bible, and then go for a swim in the Potomac River, leaving his clothes on the shore. One day, a woman journalist, who had tried to get an interview with the president, showed up and snatched the president's clothes. She would only give them back, she called out to him, if he promised to give her an interview. He didn't have much choice.

He also liked riding horses, taking long walks, and gardening, and he had the first billiards table installed in the White House.

Serving in Congress

Adams failed to win re-election in 1828, after a campaign against Andrew Jackson filled with personal attacks on both sides. But then he ran for Congress and won, becoming the first president to serve in the House of Representatives after leaving the White House. He served for 17 years, and fought hard to force Congress to find a way to solve the problem of slavery. In 1848, he collapsed and eventually died in the Capitol building.

FUN FACTS

John Quincy Adams loved science. He wanted the government to build an astronomical observatory and pay for scientific expeditions, but the public didn't share his passion, so no observatory was built during his presidency.

★★★

Adams refused to take his presidential oath of office with his hand on the Bible—he thought the Bible should be used for religious purposes only. Instead, he placed his hand on a book of laws (that included the Constitution) as he took his oath.

ANDREW JACKSON
Old Hickory

"Americans are not a perfect people, but we are called to a perfect mission."

Born
March 15, 1767
Waxhaw, North-
South Carolina
border

Political Party
Democrat

Vice Presidents
John C. Calhoun
Martin Van Buren

Wife
Rachel

Child
Andrew Jackson, Jr.
(adopted)

Pets
Several horses,
including Sam Patches,
his war horse

Simple Roots

Andrew Jackson was the first U.S. president who was born in a log cabin. His parents were poor immigrants from Northern Ireland. Very few of their neighbors in South Carolina could read, so in 1776, when he was just nine years old, Andrew read the Declaration of Independence out loud to everyone.

A Proud Scar

When the Revolutionary War broke out, Andrew and his brother joined the militia cavalry in North Carolina. He was only 13, so they made him a messenger. He was captured, and when a British officer ordered him to polish his boots, Andrew refused. The officer pulled out his sword and slashed Andrew across the face. He wore the scar proudly for the rest of his life.

Defending His Wife

In 1806, a man named Charles Dickinson insulted Jackson's wife, Rachel, so Jackson challenged him to a duel (Jackson fought several in his lifetime). Mr. Dickinson fired and his bullet lodged near Jackson's heart without killing him (doctors never got the bullet out). When Jackson fired, Mr. Dickinson did not survive. Rachel ended up dying three weeks after Jackson won the presidential election.

President Jackson

Jackson rejoined the military for the War of 1812 and clobbered the British in the Battle of New Orleans, becoming a two-star general and war hero. When he won the presidential election, he invited his rowdy friends to the celebration in the White House. The party got so loud and out of control that Jackson had to flee to a hotel across the street to get some sleep.

Jackson signed the Indian Removal Act, which let the government move Native Americans from their lands in the east to land west of the Mississippi River. He also shut down the national bank, though many people tried to stop him. Jackson was criticized for firing his enemies from government jobs and for not always doing what Congress wanted him to do—critics called him "King Andrew"—but in the end, he made the office of president stronger than it had ever been before.

FUN FACT

Jackson didn't like the people in his cabinet—his advisers—so he started meeting with a group of people he liked and trusted better. He met with these friends in the kitchen of the White House to discuss politics. They became known as the "Kitchen Cabinet," which now means a group of unofficial advisers to the president.

MARTIN VAN BUREN

Little Magician

"It is easier to do a job right than to explain why you didn't."

Born
December 5, 1782
Kinderhook,
New York

Political Party
Democrat

Vice President
Richard M. Johnson

Wife
Hannah

Children
Abraham, John,
Martin, Winfield
(died in first year),
and Smith

Pets
A pair of tiger cubs

Early Days

Even though he was the first president born in the United States (all the presidents before him were born when America was still a British colony), Martin Van Buren spoke Dutch at home. His father ran a tavern in Kinderhook, New York, between New York City and the state capital, Albany. People stopping for the night were always talking politics and young Martin listened to them with great interest. His father couldn't afford to send him to law school but did get him a job as a clerk in a law office. He taught himself the law and became a lawyer.

Van Buren's wife, Hannah, died when she was only 35, leaving him to raise their four sons on his own. The four boys helped him in his law practice and on the campaign trail when he got into politics.

Vice President and President

Van Buren liked the idea of keeping the government small. For that reason, and because he was famous for being good at settling arguments and getting people to agree (that's how he got the nickname "Little Magician"), he was noticed by Andrew Jackson, who invited him to be his vice president.

Jackson was very popular when he left office and only had to endorse Van Buren to get him elected. But soon the country's economy took a nosedive and his new nickname became "Martin Van Ruin." In the Panic of 1837, hundreds of banks and businesses failed, and thousands of people lost their jobs. Van Buren continued Jackson's mission to remove Indians from their lands in the eastern United States, and refused to admit Texas into the United States.

The two happiest days of his life, he once said, were the day he became president and the day he left the presidency. Martin Van Buren spent the rest of his days fighting against slavery.

WILLIAM HENRY HARRISON

Old Tippecanoe

"The people are the best guardians of their own rights."

Born
February 9, 1773
Charles City County,
Virginia

Political Party
Whig

Vice President
John Tyler

First Lady
Anna

Children
Elizabeth,
John (died in infancy),
Lucy, William, John,
Benjamin, Mary,
Carter, Anna,
and James

Pets
A billy goat and a cow

From Doctor to Soldier

William Henry Harrison studied medicine but became a soldier. His most famous battle was in 1811 against warriors of the Shawnee nation on the banks of the Tippecanoe River. Neither side really won the battle, but the Shawnee chief, Tecumseh, got so angry at the U.S. soldiers for giving whiskey to his people that—as legend goes—he put a curse on the government: Every president elected in a year ending in a zero would die in office.

A Modern Campaign

Harrison was nicknamed for the battle of Tippecanoe. When he ran for president, and picked John Tyler as his running mate, their slogan became "Tippecanoe and Tyler Too!" Even though he was from a wealthy, highbrow Virginia background, his campaign managers put the word out that just like Andrew Jackson, Harrison had also been born poor in a log cabin. And unlike Van Buren, who loved fine wine, Harrison preferred cider to Champagne. Guided by his advisers, Harrison also avoided talking about any important issues, a campaign tactic that worked and has been imitated ever since.

A Short-Term President

Elected in 1840, Harrison was, at 68, the oldest man to be elected president until Ronald Reagan became presidnet in 1980. Only four of his ten children lived long enough to see him win the presidency. He was inaugurated outside on a bitterly cold day, gave a speech that dragged on for an hour and 40 minutes (the longest ever), caught pneumonia, and passed away 32 days later—serving the shortest time of any U.S. president.

JOHN TYLER

His Accidency

"Wealth can only be accumulated by the earnings of industry and the savings of frugality."

Born
March 29, 1790
Charles City County,
Virginia

Political Party
Democrat and Whig

First Ladies
Letitia and Julia

Children
Mary, Robert, John,
Letitia, Elizabeth,
Anne, Alice, Tazewell,
David, John, Julia,
Lachlan, Lyon, Robert,
and Pearl

Pets
Le Beau, a greyhound;
The General, a horse

The Accidental President

When President William Henry Harrison died 32 days after being sworn into office, his vice president, John Tyler, became the first man to step into the office of president without being elected. Many people argued that he should not have all the powers of an elected president. They called him "His Accidency." Harrison's cabinet thought that they should run the country. But Tyler pushed to make sure he took full control of the job. He even refused to look at any mail sent to the "Acting President."

Tyler had already served his home state of Virginia as governor, U.S. congressman, and U.S. senator. He was popular in the southern states because he believed that states should have more say about how they ran themselves. He was kicked out of his own political party—the Whig Party—because he supported the rights of states and slavery. His stubbornness helped draw the lines that would later erupt into the Civil War. He also helped Texas join the United States as a slave state.

42

Family Life

Tyler was the first president to become a widower while in office, and the first to remarry. His second wife, Julia, was 30 years younger than he was. With his two wives, Tyler was father to 15 children, the most of any U.S. president.

Taking Sides

Just before the Civil War broke out, Tyler, broke, retired, and back at his farm in Virginia, tried to negotiate a peace treaty between the North and the South. But President Lincoln rejected all of his ideas. Tyler sided with the Confederacy and was elected to the Confederacy's Congress. He died a year later.

PRESIDENTIAL FIRSTS

John Tyler was the first president to serve without a political party. The Whigs forced him out of their party during his second year in office.

FUN FACT

Tyler was a talented violinist. His second wife would sometimes play the guitar while he played the violin. After he retired as president, he would play the violin at parties.

JAMES K. POLK

Young Hickory

"No president who performs his duties faithfully and conscientiously can have any leisure."

Born
November 2, 1795
Mecklenburg County,
North Carolina

Political Party
Democrat

Vice President
George M. Dallas

First Lady
Sarah

Pets
Horses

Manifest Destiny

James Polk believed that the United States was destined to expand to the shores of the Pacific Ocean. This belief was called "Manifest Destiny." As Polk told Congress, "The people of this continent alone have the right to decide their own destiny."

The Canadian Border

Of course, this thinking caused problems, first with the British, who were still settling Canada: An argument broke out over where the U.S. borders were in the Pacific Northwest. Polk wanted the border to be placed well within the British territory; it would have extended the United States way up into what today is Canada. When the British agreed to a border on the 49th parallel (farther south than the Americans had wanted), Polk was pleased with the compromise. The United States got present-day Oregon and Washington.

The Mexican Border

Then border problems started with Mexico over Texas. The United States declared war on Mexico. When the

Mexican-American War was over, the United States got the border it wanted for Texas and the land that would become New Mexico and California. Polk paid the Mexican government $15 million as compensation.

A Serious White House

A longtime family friend of Andrew Jackson (known as "Old Hickory"), Polk came to Washington with the nickname "Young Hickory." His wife, Sarah, was strictly religious and allowed no drinking of alcoholic beverages or dancing in the White House.

Keeping a Promise

When he ran for president, Polk promised he would serve only one term and not try to get re-elected. He kept that promise. Polk left the country two-thirds larger than when he took office. The job exhausted him; only months after retiring to his home in Tennessee, he died of cholera.

ZACHARY TAYLOR

Old Rough and Ready

"For more than half a century, during which kingdoms and empires have fallen, this Union has stood unshaken."

Born
November 24, 1784
Near Barboursville,
Virginia

Political Party
Whig

Vice President
Millard Fillmore

First Lady
Margaret

Children
Ann, Sarah, Octavia,
Margaret, Mary, and
Richard

Pet
Old Whitey, a horse

A Popular—Not Political—Man

A hero of the Mexican-American War (in the Battle of Buena Vista, his army of 6,000 defeated a Mexican force of 20,000), General Zachary Taylor was one of the most popular men in the country, but he had no experience with politics. In fact, he had never even voted in an election because he saw himself as a professional soldier, and soldiers, he believed, should not take sides in politics. He was called "Old Rough and Ready" because he used to share the hardships of war with his men and he sometimes dressed sloppily, wearing old farm clothes and a straw hat into battle.

Slavery Again

When the Whig Party picked him to run for president, he didn't think he was qualified, but he accepted because he felt it was his duty. He stepped right into the raging national argument over slavery: Should the new states of California, New Mexico, and Utah be admitted to the United States as slave states or free states? When Taylor, who owned 100 slaves himself, said that the new states should be allowed

46

to decide for themselves, both sides got mad at him.

The Northern states wanted him to stop the spread of slavery. The Southern states thought new non-slave states would make them less powerful, and they threatened to break away from the United States. Taylor warned them if they tried, he would lead the U.S. army against them.

A Short-Term President

Just 16 months after becoming president, while laying the cornerstone of the Washington Monument at a July Fourth ceremony, Taylor collapsed from heat stroke after drinking a pitcher of water and slipped into a coma. He died five days later with symptoms of cholera. More than 100,000 people lined the parade route to pay tribute to their hero.

Doctors thought Taylor got cholera from the water, or from some buttermilk and cherries he snacked on. But no matter how he died, he left the country dangerously divided and headed down the path to the Civil War.

FUN FACTS

Zachary Taylor was elected on November 7, 1848—the first time all the states voted for president and vice president on the same day.

★★★

Although Taylor was determined to stop the Southern states from breaking away from the United States, his only son, Richard, became a general in the Confederate army in the Civil War.

MILLARD FILLMORE

Last of the Whigs

"May God save the country, for it is evident that the people will not."

Born
January 7, 1800
Summerhill,
New York

Political Party
Whig

First Lady
Abigail

Children
Millard and Mary

Pets
None known,
but founded Buffalo
chapter of American
Society for the
Prevention of Cruelty
to Animals

A Poor Beginning

Born poor in a log cabin on a farm near Ithaca, New York, Millard Fillmore had to go to work instead of school to help feed his family. He taught himself to read and devoured every book he could get his hands on. He managed to put himself through six months of grammar school at the age of 17 and fell in love with his teacher, Abigail Powers, who was 19 at the time. They eventually married. A tall, handsome, and polite man, Fillmore later taught school and learned law working as a clerk. He served as a congressman and ran for governor of New York, but lost. He was elected vice president in 1848.

Becoming President

Millard Fillmore became the second vice president to become president on the sudden death of a serving president.

When he became president, the country was coming apart over the issue of slavery. Fillmore tried to hold it together by finding ways to keep both sides happy. He signed the Compromise of 1850, which, among other things, helped slave owners hunt down runaway slaves in Northern states. The law enraged everyone who was against slavery and led Harriet Beecher Stowe to write the novel *Uncle Tom's Cabin,* a story about the horrors and injustice of slavery. The book turned many Americans against slavery once and for all. It also lost Fillmore any chance of getting re-elected.

Trading with Japan

Fillmore sent Commodore Matthew Perry to Japan to persuade the Japanese, who wanted nothing to do with the United States, to start trading with America. Perry succeeded, and Japan opened its ports to U.S. shipping.

PRESIDENTIAL FIRST

Fillmore and his wife established the first permanent library at the White House.

FUN FACT

Millard Fillmore did not meet Zachary Taylor until after the presidential election, when Taylor was elected president and Fillmore was elected vice president. They did not get along well.

THE FIRST BATHTUB

Several scholars and historians claim that Millard Fillmore installed the first bathtub in the White House in 1851. It would be an interesting bit of presidential trivia if it were true—but it isn't.

Just a Joke

The false story was written in 1917 in the *New York Evening Mail* newspaper by H. L. Mencken, a writer, editor, and author who liked to play jokes on famous people and was known for his crazy sense of humor. He thought that if he made up a story about the history of the bathtub in America, it would make people forget about the fact that the country was fighting a war in Europe. But now, everyone who hears that made-up story believes that it was true!

A Made-up Story

Mencken wrote that the first bathtub in the country was an elegant wooden one put into the home of a Cincinnati businessman and the odd practice of taking a bath caught on among rich people. When word of the bathtub got out, many people thought it was just a silly toy from England made to turn ordinary Americans into fancy lords and ladies. But by bravely installing a bathtub in the White House, Mencken went on, President Fillmore really helped people get into the habit of taking regular baths.

Some years later when Mencken realized that people actually believed his story was the truth of history, he confessed to the whole joke. But even though he tried to set the record straight, people today still believe that the bathtub story is true.

The Real Truth

So what is the true story behind the White House's first bathtub? A bathing room with copper tubs and a shower was installed on the White House's first floor in 1833 or 1834 and the first permanent bathtub (on the second floor) was installed by President Franklin Pierce in 1853.

FUN FACT

President William Howard Taft was known as Big Bill because he weighed over 300 pounds and was six feet tall. None of the bathtubs in the White House were big enough for Big Bill. The solution came from an officer of the battleship *North Carolina*. When the captain heard that the president was coming to visit the ship, he had a special bathtub built for the occasion. Seven feet long and 41 inches wide, the bathtub could hold four normal-size men—and one Big Bill. After the visit President Taft had it installed in his bathroom at the White House.

FRANKLIN PIERCE

Handsome Frank

"With the Union my best and dearest earthly hopes are entwined."

Born
November 23, 1804
Hillsborough
(now Hillsboro),
New Hampshire

Political Party
Democrat

Vice President
William R. D. King

First Lady
Jane

Children
Franklin, Frank,
Robert, and Benjamin

A Rough Start

Franklin Pierce went to Bowdoin College in Maine and by his second year, he had the worst grades in his class. He made a change, though, and turned himself around, graduating third in a class that included Henry Wadsworth Longfellow and Nathaniel Hawthorne.

Giving Up Washington

At 33, he became one of the youngest U.S. senators ever. His wife, Jane, who was very strict and religious, hated the party-filled life of Washington, D.C. She made her husband resign and move back to New England. He joined the army as a private in the Mexican-American War, and by the end of the war, he had been promoted to one-star general. Friends suggested he run for president, so he did—and he narrowly won the election.

A Tragic Start in the White House

Just weeks before he was sworn in as president, Pierce's 11-year-old son, Benjamin, was killed in a train accident. The Pierces had already lost two other children. And so the first days and months in the White House were very sad for President and Mrs. Pierce. Many believe his sadness made it hard for him to do a good job as president.

PRESIDENTIAL FIRST

Franklin Pierce was the first president who gave his inauguration speech from memory.

FUN FACT

William King, Pierce's vice president, died one month after being sworn in. No one replaced him as vice president during Pierce's presidency.

Bad Decisions

Pierce tried to keep the peace between the North and the South, but he was never a very skilled politician. His biggest mistake was signing the Kansas-Nebraska Act, which let settlers in new territories decide if they wanted to allow slavery or not. The Act set off deadly riots over slavery and pushed the country closer to the brink of a civil war (a war a country fights within itself). He tried to buy Cuba, but Spain refused to sell. He did, however, add 29,000 square miles of land along the Mexican border. He was not nominated for a second term.

JAMES BUCHANAN
Old Buck

"The test of leadership is not to put greatness into humanity, but to elicit it, for the greatness is already there."

Born
April 23, 1791
Cove Gap,
Pennsylvania

Political Party
Democrat

Vice President
John C. Breckinridge

Pets
Lara, a Newfoundland dog; elephants from the King of Siam; a pair of American bald eagles

The Dred Scott Decision

James Buchanan tried running for president three times before he finally won. And it couldn't have been at a worse time.

Two days into his term, the Supreme Court (which consisted of mostly Southern judges) ruled that slaves are the property of their owners, not citizens, so they had no right to sue for their freedom. The Dred Scott Decision ignited fury among Americans, known as abolitionists, who wanted to abolish slavery.

John Brown

Among them was John Brown, a radical abolitionist who tried to start a slave revolt by stealing weapons from the armory at Harpers Ferry, Virginia, and giving them to slaves. Brown was captured and hanged, but his death made the abolitionists angrier.

Secession

By the time Buchanan's presidency ended in 1861, seven Southern states had announced that they were leaving the United States and forming a new confederacy of American states where owning slaves would be legal. Buchanan stood by helplessly as the country tore itself apart. He condemned the states for leaving, but argued that he had no power to stop them.

A Final Message

Buchanan hated slavery. He even bought slaves just to free them. But history blames him for not doing more to prevent the Civil War. On his last day in office, he sent a message to his successor: "My dear sir," he wrote, "if you are as happy on entering the presidency as I am on leaving it, then you are a happy man indeed."

The man who received that letter was Abraham Lincoln.

ABRAHAM LINCOLN

Honest Abe

"Whenever I hear anyone arguing for slavery, I feel a strong impulse to see it tried on him personally."

Born
February 12, 1809
Hodgenville, Kentucky

Political Parties
Whig and Republican

Vice Presidents
Hannibal Hamlin
Andrew Johnson

First Lady
Mary

Children
Robert, Edward,
William, and Thomas
"Tad"

Pets
Old Bob, Lincoln's
horse; Fido, a yellow
mutt

Fixing a Broken Nation

Growing up on the frontier, and as a self-taught country lawyer and politician, Abraham Lincoln spoke out against slavery his whole life. And, so, when he won the election in 1860, the pro-slavery Southern states saw what was coming. Seven Southern states left the Union, formed the Confederate States of America, and elected their own president, Jefferson Davis.

President Lincoln believed it was treason for the Southern states to quit, or secede, from the United States. He devoted himself to bringing the nation back together.

The Civil War

When Confederate troops fired on the Union's Fort Sumter in South Carolina in April 1861, Lincoln called in the army and the bloodiest chapter in American history began—the Civil War.

Lincoln ordered the navy to block Southern ports, so they couldn't export cotton or import guns. Four more states joined the Confederacy. After the Battle of Antietam, which the Northern states won, Lincoln announced his Emancipation Proclamation, which freed the slaves in the Confederate states. And in his Gettysburg Address, one of the greatest American speeches ever, he redefined the Civil War as a struggle for true freedom and a unified nation.

The Cost of War

More than 600,000 soldiers died over the next four years, but in the end, the Union won and slavery was abolished. In his oath of office, Lincoln had promised to "preserve, protect, and defend" the United States. He kept that promise and for it, many people today believe he was our greatest president ever.

A Down-to-Earth President

At six-foot-four, Lincoln was the tallest president. He spoke with a high-pitched prairie accent and used words like "thar" (for "there") and "git" (for "get"). He used to roughhouse and wrestle with his young sons Willie and Tad. And he liked to tell jokes when people would get too gloomy. "We need diversion at the White House," he once said.

The Assassination

Five days after the war ended, Lincoln and his wife went to the theater to see a play. John Wilkes Booth, a famous

Lincoln's famous Gettysburg Address—the speech he gave at the dedication of a Civil War cemetery—was only two minutes long. He wrote the speech the day before he arrived in Gettysburg. Five copies are known to exist.

actor who favored the South, slipped into the theater unnoticed, walked up to the president's box, and shot him with a pistol. Lincoln died just after seven o'clock the next morning. He was the first president to be assassinated. He was only 56 years old.

Many people wanted to pay their respects to the dead president, so his coffin was put on a funeral train to bring it to Springfield, Illinois to be buried. Buildings along the tracks were draped in black. All along the route, crowds came to watch the train go by. People were dressed in black and they cried as the car carrying the president's body made it's way slowly down the tracks. Some traveled for days just to reach the rail line and have the chance to see the funeral train as it passed by. It took 14 days for the train to get to Illinois.

A FEW WORDS NEVER FORGOTTEN

President Abraham Lincoln was asked to speak on November 19, 1863 at the dedication of the cemetery on the Civil War battlefield in Gettysburg, Pennsylvania. But Mr. Lincoln was not even the main speaker. That honor went to a famous speaker and minister from Massachusetts, Edward Everett, who later became a congressman and statesman. While Everett had two months to prepare his speech, the president didn't even get invited until two weeks before the event.

Lincoln began making a few notes about what he wanted to say only four days before going to Gettysburg, and he wrote the first copy of his speech on White House stationery the day before he left Washington. On board the train as he travelled to Pennsylvania, the president gave his speech more thought, and the night before the ceremony he finished his work, writing the last nine lines in pencil.

At the ceremony, the crowd wasn't surprised when the eloquent Everett delivered a rambling two-hour speech. The president, who wasn't feeling very well, stood before the audience with a bunch of different-size pieces of paper in his hand. He delivered his ten-sentence speech of only 270 words in less than three minutes. Because it was such a short speech, there was only a little bit of applause because the audience wasn't even sure if he was finished.

The next day, the newspapers wrote that some people were disappointed by president's speech. But most agreed that his speech was a fitting tribute to the soldiers who died at Gettysburg and a reminder to the country of the terrible cost of the Civil War.

MARY TODD LINCOLN

December 13, 1818-July 16, 1882

A Popular Girl

Mary Ann Todd was born in Lexington, Kentucky, one of seven children. Her mother died when she was a little girl. She loved school and was an excellent student, and she appeared in school plays and learned to speak French. She was outgoing and popular.

The Lawyer from Springfield

Mary met Abraham Lincoln when he was a successful lawyer in Springfield, Illinois, where she was living with her sister. She was charmed by him and he won her heart. They were married and had four children: Robert, Edward, William, and Tad. She was known as a very loving and caring mother who was devoted to her family.

Friends and Enemies

As First Lady, Mary enjoyed having parties. She loved to spend time—and often too much money—making the

White House beautiful. But she did good deeds like reading to the injured soldiers in the hospital and bringing them food and presents. Her son Tad often came with her. She had a strong will, and as First Lady, she made both friends and enemies while her husband was president.

Assassination

Five days after the end of the Civil War, President and Mrs. Lincoln went to see a play at Ford's Theatre in Washington. An actor, John Wilkes Booth, who was angry about the war, came up quietly behind the president as Mary held his hand during the play. Booth shot the president, who died the next morning. Mary Lincoln was never the same after that night.

Together Again

Her life after the president was killed was a sad one. Three of her children had already died, and only her son Robert was left to take care of her. Mary Lincoln suffered from terrible headaches and spent the rest of her life trying to find help for her poor health. When she died, she was buried next to her husband wearing the ring he gave her. On the inside of the ring was written "Eternal Love."

FUN FACTS

Mary learned French at Mentell's Academy for Girls in Lexington, Kentucky. She knew it very well and spoke French all of her life. It came in handy when she spent time living in France.

★★★

Mary Todd received 12 years of schooling—an extraordinary amount for a girl of her time. Her father strongly believed in education, not only for boys but for girls as well.

ANDREW JOHNSON
The Veto President

"The goal to strive for is a poor government but a rich people."

Born
December 29, 1808
Raleigh,
North Carolina

Political Parties
Democrat and
Unionist

First Lady
Eliza

Children
Martha, Charles,
Mary, Robert,
and Andrew

Pets
President Johnson left
food crumbs out at
night for a family of
mice living in his walls.

A Loyal Senator

When the Civil War broke out, Andrew Johnson, a senator from Tennessee, was the only Southern senator to stay at his job in Washington and not side with the South. Northerners loved him for it. It's not that he was against slavery, however (he owned slaves himself). He just believed the country should stay united. Lincoln rewarded him by making him vice president for his second term.

The Wrong Man for the Job

If Lincoln was one of our best presidents, Johnson was one of the worst. Inheriting the huge job of rebuilding the country from the ashes of war, Johnson went right to work making a mess of it. While Congress was on vacation, he started handing out pardons by the thousands. He let the South set up something called "Black Codes," which were just new ways to keep African-Americans under white people. Then Johnson started to veto laws Congress passed to protect ex-slaves and even encouraged Southern governors not to cooperate with Congress. One positive accomplishment: His administration bought Alaska from Russia for $7 million.

Impeachment

Three years into his term, Congress had had enough and put him on trial, "impeached" him, for illegally firing a government worker. He barely escaped getting kicked out of office by one vote. He left office a bitter man.

PRESIDENTIAL FIRSTS

Andrew Johnson was the first of two presidents to be impeached. Bill Clinton is the only other president who has been impeached.

★★★

Andrew Johnson was the first—and only—president to serve as senator after leaving the presidency. He became a U.S. senator from Tennessee in 1875, but died a few months after starting his term.

ULYSSES S. GRANT

Unconditional Surrender Grant

"I have never advocated war except as a means of peace."

Born
April 27, 1822
Point Pleasant, Ohio

Political Party
Republican

Vice Presidents
Schuyler Colfax
Henry Wilson

First Lady
Julia

Children
Frederick, Ulysses,
Ellen, and Jesse

Pets
Jeff Davis, Cincinnatus,
Egypt, St. Louis, Julia,
Reb, and Butcher Boy,
all horses

From the Military to the Presidency

When the Civil War ended, Ulysses S. Grant was a hero in the North. He had risen to the highest military rank since George Washington. He won the presidency in 1868, thanks to the votes of many freed slaves, but his genius in war did not automatically make him a good president.

A Name Change

Born Hiram Ulysses Grant, he was the son of a leather tanner and never had much interest in leather tanning or school. His father got him into West Point and when he signed in, they put his name down as Ulysses Simpson Grant. Grant preferred the name, since it echoed the initials of his country, so he kept the name change. His best subjects were horsemanship and math.

Civil War Hero

Grant fought in the Mexican-American War alongside his West Point classmate Robert E. Lee and later faced off against Lee in the Civil War. He accepted Lee's sword in surrender at Appomattox to end the Civil War. As the general who led the North to victory over the South, Grant was hugely popular in the North.

Too Many Scandals

As president, Grant was bewildered by the political process in Washington, D.C. and without realizing it, let several dishonest men take advantage of his trust. One scandal after another rocked his two terms. Though he was not personally involved in the scandals, he didn't always put distance between himself and those who caused the scandals, so people began to see him as weak and ineffective. Grant said that when he left office, he felt like a kid getting out of school.

The Final Years

After leaving office, Grant lost all his money in a financial scandal. Learning that he was dying of cancer, Grant spent his last years writing his memoirs to pay off his debts and leave money for his wife, working on his book up until a week before he died. The book was an instant best seller, and made half a million dollars for his surviving family.

THE MARRIAGE DIDN'T LAST

More than 30 weddings have taken place in the White House since Dolley Madison's sister, Lucy, married Thomas Todd in 1812. But the most influential occurred on May 21, 1874, when President Grant's 18-year-old daughter Nellie Grant married Algy Sartoris.

Americans wanted to know every detail about the fairytale couple. The two had traveled on a ship crossing the Atlantic Ocean. In those days, young women had chaperones whose job was to watch over them whenever handsome young men were around. Nellie's chaperones spent the trip seasick in bed, allowing the pair to meet and fall in love.

EXTRA!
THE GAZETTE
President's Daughter Weds

...al decorations ...e public rooms ...marvelous in ...y and profu- ...bove the plat- ...ere were the ...t festoons of ...est flowers- ...se's, lilies of the ...pirea and other ...varieties, lend- ...perfume to the ...that was almost ...ive in its sweet- ...Above the heads ...ouple, suspend- ...thread of flow- ...was a large bell ...l wholly of the ...f white flowers ...ent from New ...r friends. In the ...m, a bank of ...re flowers ...m oval ...ot

The wedding ceremony took place behind closed doors for invited guests only. Hundreds of candles blazed as flowers adorned the East Room of the White House, with white lilies and roses covering staircases and chandeliers. The smell of orange blossoms fresh from Florida filled the air.

Described as one of the most beautiful of all the young women who ever lived in the White House, Nellie was dressed in white, a color made popular by Queen Victoria of England. She was the only daughter in a family with three sons, and the thought of his sweet girl leaving home and going to England with her new husband brought President Grant to tears. He escorted Nellie to an altar covered with a lovely carpet, which was a gift from the sultan of Turkey. The elegant wedding was copied by many other fashionable young women of the day.

But even fairytales come to an end. The couple's marriage was troubled from the start. They had four children, but the marriage couldn't be saved. Four years after her father's death, Nellie filed for divorce and returned to the United States with her children.

Almost 40 years later, another Nellie Grant, the grand-daughter of President Grant, decided to have a much simpler wedding. She was married by a judge in New York—without even telling her mother!

FUN FACTS

In 1828, young John Adams, grandson of President John Adams and son of President John Quincy Adams, married Mary Catherine Hellen in the White House. This is the only time that a president's son has been married at the White House.

★★★

After Nellie and Algy left the White House, the president walked into his beloved daughter's room, threw himself onto her bed, and cried.

RUTHERFORD B. HAYES

Dark-Horse President

"He serves his party best who serves his country best."

Born
October 4, 1822
Delaware, Ohio

Political Party
Republican

Vice President
William Wheeler

First Lady
Lucy

Children
Birchard, James, Rutherford, Joseph, George, Fanny, Scott, and Manning

Pets
Hector and Nellie, German shepherds; the first Siamese kitten in America

A Disputed Election

Rutherford Hayes was a Union general in the Civil War. When he ran for president, he vowed he would serve only one term. That way he could focus on doing a good job and not worry about getting re-elected.

Winning the election, however, caused a scandal. In secret, his party bosses had made shady deals and rigged votes to get him elected. That's how he got the nicknames "Rutherfraud" and "His Fraudulency." His election—which was decided by Congress in the end—is one of the most disputed elections in American history.

A Hard Worker

Once in office he proved to be honest, upstanding, and hardworking. With the nation's wounds from the Civil War still healing, he had the last of the government troops removed from the South. He blocked a law that would have stopped people from immigrating to the U.S. from China. He thought it was racist. He believed that education was the best way to prosperity and harmony among a free people.

A New Kind of First Lady

Hayes' wife, Lucy, was the first First Lady to have a college degree. When her husband was a general, she accompanied him to the battle camps and helped care for the wounded and dying. She would not allow any liquor in the White House and became known by the nickname "Lemonade Lucy." Mrs. Hayes started the tradition of the annual Easter Egg Roll on the White House lawn.

PRESIDENTIAL FIRST

Rutherford Hayes was the first president to take the oath of office in the White House. Most previous presidents had taken the oath at the U.S. Capitol.

FUN FACT

Rutherford Hayes refused to campaign for Congress while he was still in the army. He won anyway.

New Inventions

Thomas Edison demonstrated his new phonograph for the Hayeses—and they kept him up until three in the morning listening to it. Hayes was also the first president to try out a telephone. "An amazing invention," he said. "But who would ever want to use one?"

JAMES A. GARFIELD

Preacher President

"A brave man is a man who dares to look the Devil in the face and tell him he is a Devil."

Born
November 19, 1831
Cuyahoga County,
Ohio

Political Party
Republican

Vice President
Chester A. Arthur

First Lady
Lucretia

Children
Eliza, Harry, James,
Mary, Irvin, Abram,
and Edward

Pet
Veto, a dog

From a Log Cabin to the White House

Probably the poorest person to ever become president, James Garfield was born in a log cabin and lost his father when he was just under two years old. His mother struggled on her own to raise the family.

When he was 17, Garfield worked on canal boats and put himself through school, eventually graduating from Williams College. He became a great teacher, preacher, and scholar. To amuse people, he would write in Greek with one hand and Latin with the other at the same time.

Garfield's Mother

He was the first president to have his mother present at his swearing-in ceremony. A tiny, frail woman, she moved into the White House and lived with the First Family. Garfield, an ex-Civil War general who was six feet tall, would personally carry his mother up and down the stairs.

President for 200 Days

As president, Garfield wanted to end the practice of handing out cushy government jobs as favors. Just four months after Garfield took office, a deranged gunman, who had been turned down for a job, sneaked up on him in a train station and shot him twice. One of the bullets lodged in Garfield's abdomen and doctors could not get it out. After two and a half months of agonizing operations and infections, Garfield died, becoming the second U.S. president to be killed by an assassin's bullet. The gunman was tried and hanged. Garfield is seen as a hero in the cause of honest government.

PRESIDENTIAL FIRST

James Garfield was the first left-handed president.

FUN FACT

Doctors couldn't find the assassin's bullet inside Garfield's body (X-rays hadn't been invented yet), so Alexander Graham Bell—known for the telephone— invented a metal detector to locate the bullet. It didn't work because it reacted to the metal in Garfield's bed, rather than the metal in his body.

CHESTER A. ARTHUR

Elegant Arthur

"Good ballplayers make good citizens."

Born
October 5, 1829
Fairfield, Vermont

Political Party
Republican

Wife
Ellen (died before
her husband became
president)

Children
William, Chester,
and Ellen

A Surprise Beginning

Chester Arthur was as shocked as anyone that President Garfield's assassin announced "Now Arthur is president!" after he gunned down Garfield.

Arthur never dreamed of becoming president. His biggest job before being vice president was running New York City's custom house, and there he was fired for "encouraging" his employees to contribute money to his political party.

An Honest President

As president, Arthur surprised everyone by turning over a new leaf and working to make government honest. He turned his back on his old friends who wanted easy government jobs and instead supported laws (known as the Pendleton Act) that required people to take a test to get a federal job. Now people had to be qualified for the government jobs they wanted; they couldn't get jobs just because they knew powerful politicians. He also helped protect people from losing their jobs because of how they voted in political elections and what party they chose to join.

New Laws and Ways of Thinking

Arthur signed the Chinese Exclusion Act, which prevented people from China from coming to the U.S. for 10 years and forbade Chinese people in the U.S. from becoming citizens.

He built up the navy and got people to start thinking about preserving the nation's wildlife and wilderness.

A Fashionable, Private Man

Because he was a very fashionable dresser, he was called "Elegant Arthur." He was said to have more than 80 pairs of trousers and would change clothes several times a day depending upon what he was doing.

He fiercely protected his personal life. "I may be President of the United States," he once said, "but my private life is nobody's damned business." He was not nominated for a second term.

PRESIDENTIAL FIRST

Chester Arthur was the first president to take the oath of office in his own home (in New York City). He was sworn into office just hours after President Garfield died. He took the oath again two days later—in a more public setting—at the U.S. Capitol.

FUN FACT

President Arthur decided to have the White House redecorated. He had over 20 wagonloads of furniture removed from the White House and sold at auction.

STEPHEN GROVER CLEVELAND
Uncle Jumbo

"Honor lies
in honest toil."

Born
March 18, 1837
Caldwell, New Jersey

Political Party
Democrat

Vice Presidents
Thomas A. Hendricks
Adlai E. Stevenson

First Lady
Frances "Frank"

Children
Ruth, Esther, Marion,
Richard, and Francis

Pets
Canaries,
mockingbirds, and
a Japanese poodle

A Quick Rise to the Presidency

Five years after the Civil War, Stephen "Big Steve" Grover Cleveland, a hard-working young lawyer, was elected sheriff of Erie County, New York. The job included the role of executioner and he personally pulled the lever to hang two murderers.

At 250-plus pounds, Cleveland was a big, honest man. As sheriff, he was tireless, fair, and evenhanded, which got noticed. He was asked to run for mayor of Buffalo, won, and before he knew it, he was governor of New York. He took on corrupt, dishonest people in government and exposed them. He became president at the age of 47.

Veto After Veto

In the White House Cleveland often answered the phone himself. He was a president who stood up to Congress. He hired and fired whom he wanted and used his veto power to block Congress 584 times, more than all of the earlier presidents combined. By doing so, he paved the way for a more powerful presidency for the 20th century, something future presidents would be grateful for.

One of the most important laws he signed during his first term was the Interstate Commerce Act, which let the government regulate railroads and other kinds of transportation. His second term was marked by a depression and labor unrest.

Many Presidential Firsts

Cleveland was the only president to be elected to two terms that were not back-to-back. He was the only president to get married in the White House. His bride, Frances or "Frank," was 28 years younger than him, famously pretty, and extremely popular. They were also the first presidential family to have a child born in the White House. The Baby Ruth candy bar was named after their daughter Ruth.

BENJAMIN HARRISON

The Human Iceberg

"The bud of victory is always in the truth."

Born
August 20, 1833
North Bend, Ohio

Political Party
Republican

Vice President
Levi P. Morton

First Lady
Caroline

Children
Russell, Mary, and Elizabeth

Pets
Dogs and a goat

Famous Relatives and Traits

He was named after his great-grandfather who signed the Declaration of Independence. His grandfather, William Henry Harrison, served as president for 30 days before dying in office. Other than that, Benjamin Harrison had few qualifications to be the president of the United States.

He preferred books to people. He was so aloof and hard to talk to that people nicknamed him "the human iceberg." One of his rivals, Theodore Roosevelt, called him "a coldblooded, narrow-minded, prejudiced, obstinate, timid, old psalm-singing Indianapolis politician."

Some Accomplishments

Even though his bumbling with the economy probably helped bring on a depression, he did do some good things as president. He supported laws to make giant companies play fair, protected forests, reached out to the lands of the Pacific, especially Hawaii, and imagined building a canal through Central America to create a waterway between the Atlantic and Pacific oceans. He also made England and Canada stop killing so many seals in the Bering Sea.

The President's Goat

President and Mrs. Harrison let their grandchildren, who lived in the White House with them, have all the pets they wanted. They had a goat named Old Whiskers hitched up to a small cart. One day the goat ran off with the kids in the cart. The president ran down Pennsylvania Avenue chasing after them.

Electricity and Baseball

Benjamin Harrison was the first president to have electricity in the White House. After he got a shock from the lights, no one wanted to touch the switches, so the lights would often stay on all night. He was also the first president to go to a baseball game (Reds 7, Senators 4; June 6, 1892). When Harrison finished his term, he told his family he felt like he had just been released from prison.

WILLIAM McKINLEY

The Major

"War should never be entered upon until every agency of peace has failed."

Born
January 29, 1843
Niles, Ohio

Political Party
Republican

Vice Presidents
Garret A. Hobart
Theodore Roosevelt

First Lady
Ida

Children
Katherine and Ida

Pets
Washington Post, a Mexican parrot, who could whistle "Yankee Doodle"

Firsts and Lasts

The last president to have served in the Civil War, William McKinley kept his army rank as his nickname for the rest of his life: "The Major."

The Spanish-American War

When McKinley became president, Cuba was still a Spanish colony, but Cubans desperately wanted their independence. Many Americans lived in Cuba, so when riots broke out, McKinley sent the battleship U.S.S. *Maine* to Havana to protect the Americans and their property. Three weeks later, the *Maine* exploded and sank in Havana Harbor. American newspapers insisted that the ship had been sunk on purpose. Even though the U.S. Navy reported that it was an accident, America declared war on Spain and the Spanish-American War began.

It didn't last long. Within four months, the United States had destroyed the Spanish fleet and taken control of Spain's global empire, including Cuba, Puerto Rico, the Philippines, and Guam. The U.S. soon added the Sandwich Islands (later renamed Hawaii). America was set to enter the 20th century as a global power.

PRESIDENTIAL FIRST

William McKinley's inauguration in 1897 was the first presidential inauguration to be filmed.

Assassination

McKinley picked a new vice president to run with him for his second term—Theodore Roosevelt, a hero from the war who was now governor of New York. McKinley won re-election and was very popular, but not with everyone.

Less than a year into his second term, McKinley was shaking hands with a line of people at a fair in Buffalo, New York. All of a sudden, a man with a bandaged hand stepped up and shot McKinley twice. He had hidden a gun in the bandage. The president took both bullets in the chest and slumped down into the arms of his bodyguard. He managed to tell his guard not to hurt the gunman, and to be careful how they gave this news to the First Lady, who suffered from delicate health.

Eight days later, McKinley died. His vice president, Theodore Roosevelt, was sworn-in as the 26th president of the United States.

FUN FACT

First Lady Ida McKinley refused to allow the color yellow in the White House. She even had the yellow flowers in the garden removed.

THEODORE ROOSEVELT

Teddy

"It is no use to preach to [children] if you do not act decently yourself."

Born
October 27, 1858
New York City,
New York

Political Party
Republican

**Vice President
(2nd Term)**
Charles Warren
Fairbanks

First Lady
Edith

Children
Alice, Theodore,
Kermit, Ethel,
Archibald, and Quentin

Pets
Horses, dogs, snakes,
lions, bears, and
a hyena

A Tough Beginning

Born to a well-to-do New York family, Theodore Roosevelt was a scrawny and sickly asthmatic boy who was picked on at school. With his father's help, he soon discovered the benefits of hard exercise and by the time he was a teenager, he was strong enough to box and wrestle at Harvard College. He graduated, married, and entered politics.

Then tragedy struck. On the same day, in the same house, his wife and his mother died within hours of each other. Theodore went out to the Western frontier to recover from his grief. He herded cattle, hunted grizzlies, and even chased outlaws.

The Rough Riders

After two years he returned to New York and married an old childhood sweetheart, Edith, and got back into public service. When the Spanish-American War broke out, Roosevelt put together a hand-picked elite cavalry unit composed of Ivy League football players, New York City policemen, and, from out West, cowboys, sheriffs, prospectors, and Native Americans. They were called the Rough Riders. In a daring raid, they captured San Juan Hill in Cuba and became heroes.

A Forward-thinking President

As president, Roosevelt filled the job vigorously with his own ideals and visions. He believed that ordinary people should not be cheated by big companies. The first environmentalist president, he set aside nearly 200 million acres for national forests, reserves, and wildlife refuges. (The "teddy bear" is named after him.) He helped end the war between Russia and Japan in 1905 by negotiating a peace treaty that was acceptable to both countries. A believer in equality, he was also the first president to invite an African-American, Booker T. Washington, to the White House for dinner.

When he left office, he went on an extended safari in Africa and collected hundreds of specimens for the Smithsonian museums.

∽ MONUMENTS TO OUR PRESIDENTS ∽

MIGHTY MOUNT RUSHMORE

Presidental Faces Carved with Dynamite

The Sioux Indians who lived in South Dakota called the mountain Six Grandfathers. The faces of four American presidents looking out over the Black Hills are carved into the face of the nearly 6,000-foot-high peak that is today called Mount Rushmore.

A Famous Sculptor

In 1924, Gutzon Borglum, a famous sculptor who created a memorial to Civil War soldiers in Georgia, was asked by officials in South Dakota to create a memorial that would bring tourists to the area. The design was supposed to be a parade of famous frontiersmen carved in rock. But Borglum thought the memorial should represent the whole country, and he proposed portraits of George Washington, Abraham Lincoln, Thomas Jefferson, and Theodore Roosevelt.

The Work Begins

He chose a site where the sun would shine on his work most of the day. Using scale models, Borglum drew the presidents, transferred his measurements to the mountain, and told his crew where to cut. Most of the sculpting was done by miners. Using jackhammers and dynamite, they removed some 400,000 tons of rock, cutting to within three inches of the final surface. So skilled were they, even in cutting the eyes and lips, that the sculptor's hammer and chisel were used very little.

When mistakes happened or when there were bad spots in the rock, Borglum changed how he arranged his figures. One cutting mistake, for example, ruined Jefferson's head, which was supposed to be on the right side of Washington. The men blasted the mistake away and then carved Jefferson on Washington's left.

Son Completes the Dream

The project took 14 years to complete and cost $1 million. Borglum died in 1941, before his dream of creating of the world's biggest sculpture was finished. His son, Lincoln, completed the final work.

Not everyone was happy with the completed monument. The Sioux Indians felt that their native land had been wrongly taken for the monument. Some people thought it spoiled the natural beauty of the area. But most people are awed by its size, beauty, and its importance.

FUN FACT
More than 2 million people visit Mount Rushmore every year.

WILLIAM H. TAFT

Big Bill

"Politics, when I am in it, makes me sick."

Born
September 15, 1857
Cincinnati, Ohio

Political Party
Republican

Vice President
James S. Sherman

First Lady
Helen "Nellie"

Children
Robert, Helen,
and Charles

Pet
Pauline, the last milk
cow kept at the
White House

A Big President

Young Bill Taft's parents put a lot of pressure on him growing up. His father had been President Grant's attorney general and he expected great things of his son. Some historians suggest that this pressure from his parents had something to do with Taft's extraordinary weight.

By the time he won the presidency, Taft weighed about 332 pounds. He had to have a new bathtub installed in the White House because he got stuck in the old one (six men had to pull him out). People joked about his size. "That Taft is a real gentleman," said one joker. "He got up on a streetcar and gave his seat to three ladies."

Big Shoes to Fill

Taft followed Theodore Roosevelt as president, and was always being compared to the popular Roosevelt. He never quite measured up, but he did accomplish several important things during his presidency. He made big businesses get in line, established the post office system, and set up the income tax system. He was the first president

to use an official auto-
mobile and had the
White House horse
stables converted into a
four-car garage.

A New Tradition

A great lover of baseball
as a boy (a strong hitter
but not a great base
runner), Taft estab-
lished a tradition of the
president throwing out
the first pitch of the baseball season.
He was also the first president to play
golf; a lot of his critics thought he should
spend more time at his desk and less on
the golf course.

The Supreme Court

Taft's dream was to be chief justice of
the Supreme Court. Eight years after
leaving the White House, President
Harding gave him the job. He did very
well there. "It is very difficult for me
to understand," said one judge, "how
a man who is so good as chief justice
could have been so bad as president."

PRESIDENTIAL FIRSTS

Taft is the only former president to give the
oath of office to other presidents. As Chief
Justice of the Supreme Court, Taft swore in
Calvin Coolidge in 1925 and Herbert Hoover
in 1929.

★★★

William Taft is the only person in American
history to be head of two branches of the
federal government: the executive branch
(president) and the judicial branch (chief
justice of the Supreme Court).

WOODROW WILSON

Professor

"I not only use all the brains that I have, but all that I can borrow."

Born
December 28, 1856
Staunton, Virginia

Political Party
Democrat

Vice President
Thomas R. Marshall

First Ladies
Ellen (died 1914) and
Edith (married 1915)

Children
Margaret, Jessie, and
Eleanor

Pet
Old Ike, a ram that
chewed cigars and
kept the White
House lawn trimmed

Early Days

The son of a minister, Woodrow had a reading disorder and didn't read well until he was 11 years old. He began working as a lawyer but got bored and decided to become a history professor instead. After working as a professor for several years, he was elected president of Princeton University. Democrats asked him to run for governor of New Jersey, and then for president.

A President for All People

As president, Wilson took on many big issues that affected everyone—child labor, the eight-hour workday, the right to strike, and the right for women to vote. He also created government agencies to take control of the money supply and keep an eye on big business.

World War I

When World War I broke out in Europe, President Wilson tried his best to keep the U.S. out of the war. But when German submarines threatened U.S. ships, he decided that America had to participate. Once in the war, he threw the full power of the U.S. at the enemy—more than one million U.S. troops were sent to Europe. At the same time he worked around the clock to find a way to get lasting peace from the sacrifice (10 million soldiers died at a cost of $300 billion). As someone who helped negotiate the treaty that ended the war, he wanted World War I to be the war that ended war for good.

With that in mind, Wilson suggested the world create an organization—a League of Nations—where every nation, big and small, would work together to maintain world peace. But he couldn't get Congress to approve it. Years later, the idea would be reborn as the United Nations.

A Great Leader

Many historians today put Woodrow Wilson in the top five of the all-time greatest presidents—along with Washington, Lincoln, and the two Roosevelts. Wilson won the Nobel Peace Prize in 1919 for his contributions to world peace.

PRESIDENTIAL FIRSTS

Woodrow Wilson was the first president to go to Europe while in office. He led the American peace delegation to Paris in 1919.

★★★

Wilson is the first—and so far only—president buried in Washington, D.C. He and his wife Edith are buried in the National Cathedral.

EDITH WILSON

October 15, 1872–December 28, 1961

The Secret President

Known as the "secret president" and the first woman to run the government, Edith Wilson took over many details of the presidency when her husband, Woodrow Wilson, had a stroke that left him unable to carry out the duties of president.

Two Marriages

The seventh of 11 children, Edith Bolling married Norman Galt when she was 24 and lived in Washington, D.C., as the wife of a well-to-do jewelry store owner.

Several years after her husband's unexpected death, she met President Wilson, whose wife had died six months earlier. Wilson was immediately charmed by her. They became quickly engaged—although they kept the engagement a secret because it came so soon after his wife's death—and married only nine months after they met.

The President's Companion

Edith Wilson became her husband's constant companion and personal assistant. She traveled to

Europe with him, golfed with him, and sat next to him at important White House dinners. He shared secret government information with her.

When the United States entered the war in 1917, the First Lady got involved with the war effort. She helped feed soldiers leaving for the war, rationed food, and even saved manpower and money by using sheep to keep the White House lawn trimmed.

The President's Stroke

After Wilson's stroke in 1919, the first lady hid the severity of his condition. She controlled who saw the president, so his cabinet, newspaper reporters, and the American people didn't know how sick he really was. She screened his mail, decided what was important enough for him to see, and answered questions for him.

Always Mrs. Wilson

President Wilson never fully recovered from his stroke, and he retired from politics when his term was over. He died three years after he left the White House. Edith Wilson spent the rest of her life representing him at special occasions, even riding in President Kennedy's inaugural parade. She died on her husband's birthday in 1961.

FUN FACT

Edith Wilson owned and drove an electric car.

WARREN G. HARDING

Wobbly Warren

"I'm not fit for this office and never should have been here."

Born
November 2, 1865
Blooming Grove,
Ohio

Political Party
Republican

Vice President
Calvin Coolidge

First Lady
Florence "Duchess"

Stepchild
Marshall Eugene
DeWolfe

Pets
Laddie Boy,
an Airedale terrier;
Old Boy, an English
bulldog; canaries

What Does a President Do?

Called by many the worst president the United States has ever had, Warren Harding worked hard to earn the title. His campaign slogan was "Back to Normalcy," inviting Americans to turn back the clock to the simpler times before World War I—and before all the accomplishments of Woodrow Wilson.

Unfortunately, America took him up on it, and Harding won by a landslide. Once in office, Harding realized he really didn't know what the job of president was. Never a deep thinker, Harding behaved as if all he had to do was look and act presidential, avoiding big issues whenever they came up. "I don't know what to do or where to go," he told a friend. "Somewhere there must be a book that talks all about it."

A Few Good Men

Luckily, Harding had appointed three or four good, solid men to his cabinet, who kept the country from falling apart— men like Calvin Coolidge, Andrew Mellon, Charles Evans Hughes, and Herbert Hoover. But still, the good-natured and trusting "Wobbly Warren" let a gang of dishonest scoundrels into his administration, and they got busy taking bribes and breaking laws to make themselves rich. Harding would play poker with these men late into the night, drinking liquor (even though alcohol was illegal then). Harding even lost the White House dishes in a card game.

PRESIDENTIAL FIRST

Warren Harding was the first president to visit the state of Alaska.

A Mysterious Death

When the word got out that many of these dishonest men were about to be brought to trial, one fled the country, two committed suicide, and Harding, on a trip out west, got sick from what seemed to be food poisoning and died of heart failure in San Francisco. People immediately started to suspect that he had been murdered, although it could never be proved.

FUN FACT

Harding kept plenty of alcohol in the White House for his late-night poker games—even though he voted for Prohibition (which outlawed the sale of alcohol) when he was a senator.

CALVIN COOLIDGE
Silent Cal

"**Any man who does not like dogs and want them about does not deserve to be in the White House.**"

Born
July 4, 1872
Plymouth Notch,
Vermont

Political Party
Republican

Vice President
Charles Gates Dawes

First Lady
Grace

Children
John and Calvin

Pets
Rebecca and Reuben, raccoons; dogs: Palo Alto, King Cole, Blackberry, Rough, Ruby, Boston Beans

Taking the Oath

Vice President Calvin Coolidge was visiting his father in Vermont when President Harding died in San Francisco. The news reached them at night and Coolidge's father, who was a justice of the peace, administered the oath of office to his son, who immediately went back to bed.

A Calm Leader

A quiet, witty, redheaded New Englander, Coolidge was the kind of calm and wholesome president the country needed after Harding's escapades. Trained as a lawyer and a former governor of Massachusetts, "Silent Cal" was famous for not talking. Once a high society lady seated next to him said, "You must talk to me, Mr. Coolidge. I made a bet today that I could get more than two words out of you." Coolidge replied: "You lose."

Boom Times in America

During Coolidge's terms in office, the country was going through good times, often called the Roaring Twenties. Coolidge believed the government should not interfere with the strong economy. He gave tax cuts to the rich and did little to help farmers who

were going out of business. People put more and more of their money into the stock market, even if they were risking too much of it. Coolidge didn't try to stop the risk-taking; he believed it wasn't the president's job to try to control the stock market.

A Happy White House

The Coolidges held lots of parties in the White House. As quiet and reserved as President Coolidge was, his wife, Grace, was talkative and bubbly. She called herself the "national hugger." Trained in sign language and lip reading to communicate with the deaf, she was a personal friend of Helen Keller.

Coolidge slept more than any president, about ten hours a day, including afternoon naps. But many think he was also asleep at the switch and believe his passive approach to being president set the stage for the economic disaster that followed his time in office. He decided not to run for re-election, simply saying, "I do not choose to run for president in 1928."

HERBERT HOOVER

Chief

"Children are our most valuable natural resource."

Born
August 10, 1874
West Branch, Iowa

Political Party
Republican

Vice President
Charles Curtis

First Lady
Lou

Children
Herbert and Allan

Pets
Patrick, an Irish wolf-hound; Sonnie and Big Ben, fox terriers; Yukon, an Eskimo dog; two alligators that wandered around the White House

A Happy and Sad Childhood

When Herbert Hoover was born, his father, the village blacksmith, had such high hopes for him that he marched through town announcing, "We have another General Grant in our house!"

"Bert" Hoover grew up in Iowa, where he learned how to trap rabbits and catch fish. When he was six, his father died and his mother died four years later. Orphaned, Bert was separated from his brother and sister and sent to live with an uncle in Oregon.

A Rich Geologist

Hoover went to Stanford, a new college in California, and studied geology and mining. Before long, he was a self-made millionaire, traveling all over the world. He helped evacuate Americans from Europe before World War I broke out and took charge of food rationing in the United States during the war.

Difficult Times

Hoover was very popular when he ran for president and won easily. But a few months later, the stock market crashed and the Great Depression began. Banks failed, businesses were ruined, people lost their jobs, and everyone blamed Hoover. After a while he gave banks and businesses loans, but refused to give money directly to unemployed and homeless people, which made him seem uncaring about the suffering caused by the depression.

None of what he tried to do improved the economy and by the time his term was ending, 14 million people were without work. Many lived in shacks and tent villages called "Hoovervilles" in extreme poverty. Hitchhikers held signs that read: "If you don't give me a ride, I'll vote for Hoover." He was not re-elected.

Helping Others

Although history says Hoover was not a good president, he was a great humanitarian. After World War II, he helped get food to war-torn Europe. For 25 years he ran the Boys Clubs of America, because he always had special concern for "the boys of the city streets."

FRANKLIN D. ROOSEVELT
FDR

"When you get to the end of your rope, tie a knot and hang on."

Born
January 30, 1882
Hyde Park, New York

Political Party
Democrat

Vice Presidents
John N. Garner
Henry A. Wallace
Harry S. Truman

First Lady
Anna Eleanor

Children
Anna, James, Elliott, Franklin, John, and a son who died young

Pets
Fala, a Scottish terrier, and other dogs

The Great Depression

When Franklin Roosevelt became president in the middle of the Great Depression, millions of Americans were out of work, poor, and homeless. And there was no end in sight to their misery and suffering. In his first speech, FDR gave hope. "This great nation will endure as it has endured, will revive, and will prosper," he said. "The only thing we have to fear is fear itself."

He charged into the job, starting many programs that gave people a "new deal" and put them to work. Believing that the federal government should help the needy, he provided aid to the unemployed, farmers, businessmen, and bankers. Social Security payments were created to help sick, elderly, and disabled Americans. His wife, Eleanor, worked tirelessly to help the poor and inspired many Americans to do the same. After four years, the economy seemed to be improving, and he won re-election.

A New Challenge

In Roosevelt's second term, a new war broke out in Europe when Hitler's

Nazi Germany invaded Poland. Even though the U.S. stayed out of the war at first, American factories made weapons and war supplies to help England, France, and other friends fighting Germany. Without entering the war, the U.S. was able to support the war effort—and put more Americans back to work.

Pearl Harbor

When Japanese planes attacked American ships anchored at Pearl Harbor, Hawaii, on December 7, 1941, the United States entered World War II and fought it for the next four years. FDR was a true commander in chief, studying battle plans, appointing field commanders, and, using the radio to talk to Americans, keeping the nation solidly behind the war. His radio broadcasts gave Americans confidence and hope during the darkest days of the war.

A Disabled President

FDR became the only U.S. president to win four straight elections. He also was the only physically disabled president—he contracted polio when he was 39 and learned to get around with braces and crutches, and, eventually, in a wheelchair. Because photographers agreed not to publish

PRESIDENTIAL FIRST

FDR was the first president to appoint a woman to his cabinet. In 1933, he chose Frances Perkins as his Secretary of Labor.

photographs of him in a wheelchair, most people didn't know about his condition.

FUN FACT

Roosevelt loved to collect stamps. His stamp collection included over a million stamps at the time of his death (though many weren't worth much money).

Big Successes

When FDR died suddenly of a brain hemorrhage, the country was at work again, victory in the World War II was just around the corner, and the United States had a new place of respect in the world. He died as one of the most beloved, admired, and respected leaders in history.

In 1997, a memorial to him was unveiled at the National Mall in Washington, D.C. Only three other presidents have been given the same honor— Washington, Jefferson, and Lincoln.

ON THE MONEY

The last time you broke open your piggy bank to spend your treasure trove of coins, did you look at the images of the U.S. presidents that appear on them? Here are the values of presidential U.S. coins in circulation today, the president on the front of them, what appears on the back, and the date the coin was first issued:

Penny	Abraham Lincoln	The Lincoln Memorial	1909
Nickel	Thomas Jefferson	Monticello	2006
Dime	Franklin D. Roosevelt	Olive Branch, Torch, and Oak Branch	1946
Quarter	George Washington	American Bald Eagle	1932
Half-Dollar	John F. Kennedy	The Presidential Seal	1964
Dollar	Dwight D. Eisenhower	Moon, Eagle	1971

FUN FACT

★ The Lincoln cent was issued in 1909 to commemorate the 100th anniversary of Abraham Lincoln's birth.

★ The original image of Thomas Jefferson, created by Felix Schlag, appeared on the nickel from 1938 to 2006. The design was chosen from among those created by 390 artists.

★ When Franklin Roosevelt died in 1945, the Treasury Department received many requests to honor the late president by placing his portrait on a coin. In 1946, the dime with John R. Sinnock's portrait was released on FDR's birthday, January 30.

★ The portrait of George Washington by John Flanagan, which appears on quarters minted since 1932, was selected for the 200th anniversary of our first president's birth.

★ Legend says that George Washington donated some of his personal silver to the Mint for making early coins.

ELEANOR ROOSEVELT

October 11, 1884–November 7, 1962

A New Kind of First Lady

Married to her fifth cousin, Franklin Delano Roosevelt, Eleanor Roosevelt worked hard to improve living and working conditions for women, working people, and the poor, pushed for civil rights, and represented her husband in her travels around the country and the world.

Early Years

Anna Eleanor Roosevelt had an unhappy childhood. Her mother and father died before she was ten. She lived with her grandmother until age 15, when she was sent to school in England. When she returned to New York, she volunteered to teach at a shelter, where she saw the terrible living and working conditions many poor people faced. She also visited their overcrowded apartment buildings.

A Hard-Working First Lady

Several years after she married Franklin Roosevelt, he contracted polio. She encouraged him to continue his political career, and he became governor of New York and then president. Because he couldn't walk, she became his eyes and ears, traveling to inspect hospitals

and prisons, visit wounded soldiers, make speeches (even though she was very shy), and show workers and poor people that the president understood their problems. She also pressured her husband to help improve the lives of women, African-Americans, and poor people.

She wrote a column called "My Day," about her life as First Lady, as well as magazine articles and books. Eleanor Roosevelt held weekly press conferences (allowing only female reporters—who usually weren't allowed in presidential press conferences—to attend), and was the first First Lady to address a national political convention.

Life After the White House

President Truman made Eleanor Roosevelt a U.S. delegate to the United Nations after her husband died. President Kennedy asked her to serve on a committee about women. When she died, Truman called her the "First Lady of the World." She is still an inspiration to civil rights and women's rights leaders today.

FUN FACT

Eleanor Roosevelt resigned from a group that wouldn't let Marian Anderson, an African-American singer, give a concert in a Washington, D.C. auditorium. She helped plan a free concert for the singer at the Lincoln Memorial, which was attended by more than 75,000 people.

HARRY S. TRUMAN

Give 'Em Hell Harry

"The best way to give advice to your children is to find out what they want and then advise them to do it."

Born
May 8, 1884
Lamar, Missouri

Political Party
Democrat

Vice President
Alben William Barkley

First Lady
Elizabeth "Bess"

Child
Margaret

Pets
Feller and Mike, dogs

Unexpected Event

Three months after Harry Truman became vice president, he became president. It felt like "the moon, the stars, and all the planets had fallen on me," he said.

The Atomic Bomb

President Truman was immediately faced with a decision perhaps more difficult than any president had ever faced before. American scientists had created a new kind of bomb, the likes of which the world had never seen. FDR had authorized its secret development, but Truman, and the rest of the world, didn't even know it existed. The atomic bomb's destructive power was terrifying.

If Truman decided to let World War II continue, the United States would have had to invade Japan to stop the fighting and hundreds of thousands more soldiers, on both sides, would have died. If Truman decided to use the atomic bomb, Japan would have to surrender, and all those lives would be spared. Truman ordered two atomic bombs dropped on Japan—one on Hiroshima and one on Nagasaki—and the war came to an end within days.

New Challenges

When millions of soldiers came back home to the United States, Truman had to figure out how to educate them and train them for work. He also had to help rebuild the world. He saw that Communism was spreading and wanted to stop it. He came up with the Truman Doctrine, which promised countries fighting Communism that the U.S. would help them with economic and military aid. He also implemented the Marshall Plan, which helped rebuild European cities that had been destroyed by the war. Tension between the U.S. and the Communist Soviet Union grew and grew until it turned into the Cold War, which would occupy U.S. presidents for the next 30 years.

Family Loyalty

Truman was a devoted family man. When a newspaper writer criticized his daughter Margaret, a singer, President Truman wrote this note to him: "Someday I hope to meet you. When that happens, you'll need a new nose."

Retirement

Truman decided not to run for president again, and retired to Independence, Missouri. He died at the age of 88.

DWIGHT D. EISENHOWER

Ike

"Only Americans can hurt America."

Born
October 14, 1890
Denison, Texas

Political Party
Republican

Vice President
Richard M. Nixon

First Lady
Marie "Mamie"

Children
Doud Dwight
and John

Pet
Heidi, a Weimaraner

Military Hero

Growing up with five brothers, "Ike" Eisenhower knew how to fight—and how to make peace.

One of America's greatest military commanders, Eisenhower was Supreme Commander of the Allied troops that invaded France on D-Day in 1944, the military operation that marked the beginning of the end of World War II.

A Call to the Presidency

When Eisenhower came home, he was such a popular and beloved hero that President Truman privately suggested that they run together in 1948—but with Eisenhower as president and Truman as vice president.

Instead, Eisenhower became president of Columbia University and ran for the White House as a Republican in 1952. Campaign buttons read: "I like Ike!" And a lot of people did. He won in a landslide.

Keeping Peace

Eisenhower ended the war in Korea but continued to oppose the spread of

Communism across the world. He tried to ease tensions with the Soviet Union, even meeting with the Soviet leader, but the Cold War only got worse.

He also worked for cooperation between people at home. When the Arkansas governor refused to let African-American schoolchildren enter an all-white school in Little Rock, Arkansas, and mobs threatened violence, Eisenhower sent federal troops to keep the peace—and escort the children into school.

At Home at the White House

Eisenhower loved fishing and playing cards, but his favorite activity was golf. He had a putting green installed behind the White House so he could practice.

His dog, Heidi, once made such a mess in the White House that she was sent home to Pennsylvania. After a while, however, the president missed her so much that he sent a limousine to bring her back.

Ike left office one of the best-liked presidents ever.

CAMP DAVID

COUNTRY HOME FOR PRESIDENTS

Camp David, the president's country home, is located in Catoctin Mountain Park in Maryland, about 60 miles from the White House. It was once a family camp for people who worked in Washington, D.C. Covered with trees and high in the mountains, the spot provides a cool place in the summer where the president can escape from his busy job.

Plenty to Do

Camp David was first named Shangri-La by President Franklin Roosevelt, but President Eisenhower later named it David in honor of his father and grandson. The main lodge was made to look like President Roosevelt's winter home in Georgia. Camp David has a one-hole golf course. It also has two swimming pools, a tennis court, a two-lane bowling alley, a skeet range, and a basketball court. There is even an Evergreen Chapel.

A Place for Visitors

Camp David has often been used as a place where leaders visiting the U.S. from other countries can stay and have meetings. Prime Minister Winston Churchill of Great Britain, Egyptian President Anwar al-Sadat, and Israeli Prime Minister Menachem Begin are a few of the leaders who came to Camp David. Every president since Franklin Roosevelt has used Camp David. President Truman's favorite sport was walking, and he spent long hours wandering the mountain trails—with a secret service agent right behind him.

And Families

The presidents' families could also stay at Camp David. President Kennedy and his family went horseback riding and played sports there. President Nixon had several new buildings built, complete with modern conveniences, and he held family get-togethers there. President Gerald Ford liked to ride his snowmobile around Camp David in the winter. President Ronald Reagan spent more time at Camp David than any other president. He liked horseback riding and working in the woodworking shop. President George H. W. Bush's daughter, Dorothy, was the first to be married there in 1992.

In keeping with the geography of the forests on Catoctin Mountain Park, all of the guest cottages and most of the buildings are named after trees, including Aspen, the Presidential Lodge.

FUN FACT

President Nixon installed microphones at Camp David in 1972 so he could record conversations.

JOHN F. KENNEDY

Jack

"Man is still the most extraordinary computer of all."

Born
May 29, 1917
Brookline, Massachusetts

Political Party
Democrat

Vice President
Lyndon B. Johnson

First Lady
Jacqueline "Jackie"

Children
Caroline, John Jr., and Patrick (died in infancy)

Pets
Charlie, a Welsh terrier; Tom Kitten; Macaroni, Caroline's pony; Zsa Zsa, a rabbit; Sardar, a horse

Camelot

President for only some 1,000 days before a gunman ended his young life, Jack Kennedy left one of the most lasting impressions of any president in history. Handsome, charming, and eloquent, he inspired a whole generation to take up the challenges of a "New Frontier." The glamour and idealism of his presidency earned those years the nickname "Camelot," after King Arthur's mythical court.

Hero and Politician

Born into a rich family, Kennedy was captain of a small PT (patrol torpedo) boat in the Pacific during World War II. One night, while the boat drifted and the crew slept, a Japanese destroyer rammed the PT boat and the whole crew ended up in the water. Kennedy led his men on a three-mile swim through shark-infested waters to safety, towing a wounded crewman by holding the strap from his life vest in his teeth.

Kennedy came home a hero and went into politics. After serving in Congress, he became the youngest man ever to run for president, and he won. He asked the world, including our enemies, never to give up on peace. He told Americans to "ask not what your country can do for you—ask what you can do for your country."

Opportunities and Crises

Kennedy passed a law giving equal rights to minorities and created the Peace Corps, which sent Americans to work for free in poor foreign countries. He promised to put a man on the moon within nine years (it happened). In 1962, when he discovered that the Soviet Union had put nuclear missile bases in Cuba (not far from the U.S.), he ordered a blockade around the island. For 13 days the U.S. and the Soviet Union came close to nuclear war—until the Soviet Union agreed to take away the missiles. Kennedy also started sending troops into a small country in Asia called Vietnam.

The Assassination

In an event that still shocks and saddens the world, President Kennedy was assassinated by a lone gunman, Lee Harvey Oswald, in Dallas on November 22, 1963. He died at age 46, after being president for only 1,037 days.

JACQUELINE KENNEDY

July 28, 1929–May 19, 1994

An American Role Model

Beautiful and elegant, Jackie Kennedy turned the White House into a living museum, publicly supported American artists and musicians, and showed great strength and grace when her husband was assassinated.

A Young First Lady

Jacqueline Bouvier was born into a wealthy family in Southampton, New York. After a privileged childhood in New York and Washington, D.C., she became a photographer for a newspaper in the nation's capital. She met John F. Kennedy, a handsome U.S. congressman from Massachusetts, at a dinner party and married him in 1953 at the age of 24. At 31, she moved into the White House with her two young children and her husband, the newly elected president.

Favorite Projects

The First Lady began restoring the White House, making sure that the furniture, paintings, and decorative arts (like candlesticks and pottery) reflected America's past. She hosted plays, ballet, jazz, and other cultural events at the White House, inviting America's most talented performers

into her home. She even gave a tour of the White House that was shown on television. Her efforts to celebrate American history and artistic talent brought new attention to American culture.

Tragedy Strikes

Jackie Kennedy was sitting next to her husband in the presidential limousine when he was shot. Stunned by what had happened, she stood bravely in her blood-spattered pink suit next to Lyndon Johnson as he took the oath of office after the president died. She gracefully and courageously led the country in mourning the loss of her husband.

Life After the White House

She moved back to New York City and five years later married Aristotle Onassis, a wealthy Greek businessman. She began a career as a book editor after his death in 1975, and worked hard to preserve Grand Central Terminal. Fashionable and elegant until the end, she died of cancer at her New York City home at the age of 64.

FUN FACT

So many women wanted to copy Jackie Kennedy's stylish outfits that department stores dressed mannequins to look like her in the style of clothes that she wore.

LYNDON B. JOHNSON

LBJ

"You aren't learning anything when you're talking."

Born
August 27, 1908
Stonewall, Texas

Political Party
Democrat

Vice President
Hubert H. Humphrey

First Lady
Claudia "Lady Bird"

Children
Lynda Bird
and Luci Baines

Pets
Beagles, a collie; Yuki,
a stray mutt found
in a gas station and
adopted

The Great Society

The first president ever sworn into office aboard an airplane, Lyndon Johnson asked the country to honor President Kennedy's memory by continuing the good work he started. Americans would create "The Great Society," he said. The United States would end racial hatred, clean up the air and water, and most important of all, declare an all-out "war on poverty."

LBJ Everywhere

Johnson, or "LBJ," was a big, no-nonsense Texan who spoke with a drawl and often wore a Stetson cowboy hat. He had a family tradition that gave everyone the same initials: his wife, Claudia, was nicknamed "Lady Bird," and their two daughters were named Lynda Bird and Luci Baines.

Early Successes

LBJ was very good at politics and got many of his Great Society ideas put into law. He succeeded in getting anti-poverty, civil rights, and voting rights laws passed, making him popular and winning him the next election easily.

Two Crises

Johnson faced two crises that overshadowed his presidency. The biggest crisis was the war in Vietnam, which was growing out of control abroad and pitting Americans against each other at home. Anti-war protesters held demonstrations, sometimes violent, across the country. In addition, race riots erupted in several cities. It was one of the most turbulent times in our history.

By the time Johnson was up for re-election, there were a half-million U.S. soldiers in Vietnam, and many were dying. The U.S. had dropped more bombs in Vietnam than in all of Europe in World War II. And no victory was in sight.

Refusing Re-election

Discouraged and with a heavy heart, Johnson refused to run again and retired to his ranch in Texas. Lady Bird Johnson continued to work tirelessly for the poor and to beautify America.

PRESIDENTIAL FIRSTS

Lyndon Johnson was the first (and only) president sworn in by a woman. Federal judge Sarah T. Hughes administered the oath on Air Force One, the president's plane, about two hours after Kennedy was assassinated.

★★★

Johnson was the first president to nominate an African-American, Thurgood Marshall, to the Supreme Court.

113

RICHARD M. NIXON

Tricky Dick

"I am not a crook."

Born
January 9, 1913
Yorba Linda,
California

Political Party
Republican

Vice Presidents
Spiro T. Agnew
Gerald R. Ford

First Lady
Thelma "Pat"

Children
Patricia "Tricia" and
Julie

Pets
Checkers, a spaniel;
Vicky, a poodle;
Pasha, a terrier;
King Timahoe, an
Irish setter

A Strong Start

After his graduation from Duke Law School, Nixon's rise in politics was like a meteor: congressman in 1946, senator in 1950, vice president in 1952. If it had not been for a few votes in 1960, he would have beaten Kennedy and been the 35th president.

Instead, he ran for governor of California, but lost. Announcing that he was getting out of politics, he said to the press, "You won't have Nixon to kick around anymore, because, gentlemen, this is my last press conference."

Back to Politics

It wasn't his last press conference, of course. Nixon came back and won the presidency in 1968 and was in the White House on July 20, 1969, when astronaut Neil Armstrong put the first human footprints on the moon.

Nixon was very clever when it came to getting votes. Some said too clever and gave him the nickname "Tricky Dick." He got elected president by promising to end the war in Vietnam, but the war dragged on and on.

Foreign Problems and Solutions

Nixon brought troops home little by little, but increased the bombing of Vietnam. "Peace is at hand," the White House kept telling the public. Anti-war protests got louder and louder and 20,000 more Americans died before Nixon finally got U.S. soldiers out of Vietnam completely.

Nixon started talking with the leaders of Communist giants China and the Soviet Union, even visiting both countries in order to improve relations with them.

Watergate

Nixon was expected to win re-election easily in 1972. But in order to be sure of success, his assistants broke into the offices of the Democratic National Committee at the Watergate office building in Washington, D.C, to spy on his competition. When his spies were caught, most of them lied about what they had been doing. So did Nixon. He resigned in disgrace in August 1974 rather than be impeached—get put on trial—by the Senate.

"Always remember," he said, "others may hate you, but those who hate you don't win unless you hate them. And then you destroy yourself."

PRESIDENTIAL FIRST

In 1972, Richard Nixon was the first president to visit a country (China) that had not been officially recognized by the United States government.

FUN FACTS

Nixon was the first president to speak with a man on the moon.

★★★

Nixon welcomed Elvis Presley to the White House in 1970. Elvis had written Nixon a letter suggesting he become a "federal agent-at-large" in the Bureau of Narcotics and Dangerous Drugs. He was given a BNDD badge (but not the job).

GERALD R. FORD
Jerry

"I am a Ford, not a Lincoln."

Born
July 14, 1913
Omaha, Nebraska

Political Party
Republican

First Lady
Elizabeth Anne
"Betty"

Children
Michael, John, Steven,
and Susan

Pet
Liberty, a golden
retriever, who gave
birth to a litter of
puppies in the
White House

A Fresh Start

Gerald Ford became president when Richard Nixon resigned in disgrace. "My fellow Americans," Ford said, entering the White House, "Our long national nightmare is over." The dark days of people not trusting their president were over. He made it his goal to restore people's faith in America.

A Scholar-Athlete

Ford knew something about scoring goals. A star football player, he was an All-American center and linebacker for the University of Michigan who led his team to two undefeated, championship seasons. "I had pro offers from the Detroit Lions and Green Bay Packers," he said later. "If I had gone into professional football, the name Jerry Ford might have been a household word today."

Instead he went to Yale Law School, paying his tuition by taking positions as Yale's boxing coach and assistant football coach. He graduated in the top quarter of his class, even though he had been so busy with his coaching duties.

Political Career

Ford served on an aircraft carrier in the Pacific in World War II and then became a Michigan congressman, serving for nearly 25 years. His biggest hope was to be Speaker of the House, but he had to settle for vice president (appointed when Nixon's vice president resigned) and then president (when Nixon resigned).

Ford destroyed his chances for continuing as president when he pardoned Richard Nixon for any crimes he may have committed against the United States during his presidency. Some people thought something fishy was going on. But Ford did it, he said, because it was the right thing to do, to help heal the country.

Personal Life

Ford often said that the thing he was proudest of in his life was making the rank of Eagle Scout in the Boy Scouts. He always kept a copy of the Boy Scout manual on his desk throughout his career. When he died in 2006, more than 400 Eagle Scouts formed an honor guard at his state funeral.

PRESIDENTIAL FIRST

Gerald Ford was the first (and only) president who was not elected either vice president or president but served as both.

FUN FACT

Gerald Ford was born with the name Leslie Lynch King, Jr. His parents separated just weeks after he was born, and after the divorce his mother married Gerald Rudolff Ford. They called her son Gerald Rudolff Ford, Jr. He legally changed his name (using the more common spelling of Rudolph) when he was 22 years old.

BETTY FORD

April 8, 1918–July 8, 2011

Betty Ford was a First Lady who was unafraid to speak out on the important issues of the day. The way she took care of her personal problems was her greatest contribution to the nation.

Off to Washington

Elizabeth Anne "Betty" Ford grew up in Michigan. When she was eight, she began to study dance and dreamed of becoming a dancer. She was introduced to Gerald Ford, Jr., a college football star who went to Harvard and became a lawyer. They began dating and soon were married. When Jerry announced his candidacy for Congress, Betty jumped in to help with his campaign for Congress—and he won! When President Richard Nixon resigned in 1974, Gerald Ford, who was vice president, took the oath of office as the new president.

Outspoken

As First Lady, Betty Ford spoke out in favor of equal rights for women and her support for a woman to serve on the U.S. Supreme Court. Soon after becoming First Lady, Betty found out that she had breast cancer. Her openness about the disease and the importance of getting early treatment gave other women hope.

Needed Help

When President Ford lost the presidency, Betty was very sad. She began to drink too much alcohol and take too many drugs for her back pain, and she soon realized that she needed help. She checked herself into the Long Beach Naval Hospital and her experience there led her to open the Betty Ford Treatment Center in California. She was open and honest about her treatment. Because Betty Ford spoke out about her problems, she made it easier for other people to get the help they needed—and probably saved many lives.

FUN FACT

When she was a teenager, Betty Ford studied dance with the famous dance teacher, Martha Graham. She was such a talented dancer that she was chosen to dance at Carnegie Hall!

JAMES EARL CARTER

Jimmy

"Wherever life takes us, there are always moments of wonder."

Born
October 1, 1924
Plains, Georgia

Political Party
Democrat

Vice President
Walter Mondale

First Lady
Rosalynn

Children
John "Jack,"
James Earl III "Chip,"
Jeffrey "Jeff," and Amy

Pets
Grits, a collie; Misty
Malarky Ying Yang, a
Siamese cat

Before Politics

Jimmy Carter grew up on his family's peanut farm in Georgia. He studied nuclear physics at the U.S. Naval Academy at Annapolis and worked on a nuclear submarine. When his father died in 1953, Carter went home to run the farm and soon got into politics.

The Outsider

When Carter ran for president, people liked him because he was an "outsider" in Washington. Voters were tired of all the wheelers and dealers in the government and wanted someone new who wasn't "connected." Carter was a born-again Christian with very high moral standards.

World Problems

Unfortunately for the new president, a worldwide energy crisis was making gas prices skyrocket out of control. Cars had to wait in long lines just to buy gas. And it got more expensive than ever to borrow money to buy a house.

In Iran, protesters stormed the U.S. embassy in November 1979 and took 52 American diplomats hostage, holding them as prisoners. Carter worked around the clock to get them free, but couldn't. After 444 days—and on Carter's last day as President—the hostages were released.

An Outsider's Problems

Not being a Washington "insider" worked against President Carter. He had trouble getting Congress to go along with many of his ideas. And international and domestic difficulties just didn't seem to get any better. He lost re-election.

The Nobel Prize

An extremely intelligent, decent, and sincere man, Carter was the third U.S. president to be awarded the Nobel Peace Prize. In 2002 he was awarded the honor for forging a 1978 peace treaty between warring sides in the Middle East.

"War may be a necessary evil," he said. "But no matter how necessary, it is always an evil, never a good. We will not learn to live together in peace by killing each other's children."

An Active Former President

After leaving the White House, he and Mrs. Carter worked to build homes for the homeless, often taking up hammer and nails and doing the carpentry them-selves. Carter also actively worked for human rights causes around the world.

121

RONALD REAGAN
The Great Communicator

"Don't be afraid to see what you see."

Born
February 6, 1911
Tampico, Illinois

Political Party
Republican

Vice President
George H. W. Bush

First Lady
Nancy

Children
Maureen, Michael,
Patricia, Ronald,
and Christine
(died in infancy)

Pets
Lucky, a Bouvier des
Flandres; Rex, a King
Charles spaniel

An Actor First

At 69, former movie star Ronald Reagan was the oldest president ever to enter the White House. He joked: "Thomas Jefferson once said, 'We should never judge a president by his age, only by his works.' And ever since he told me that, I stopped worrying."

The Actor

Called the Great Communicator, Reagan was perfectly at ease in front of cameras and large crowds. His years in Hollywood had prepared him for one of the greatest demands of the job: winning people over. "How can a president not be an actor?" he asked.

He made more than 50 movies for Warner Brothers Studios, usually cast as the wholesome all-American kid. Only Errol Flynn received more fan mail than he did. He then went to work for General Electric as a television host and became familiar to even more Americans.

Political Life

When he entered politics, he rose quickly, serving as governor of California for eight years. He beat his opponent in his first run for governor by almost a million votes.

When he ran for president, he campaigned on his belief that government was too big, and that reducing taxes for the rich would help everyone when their wealth "trickled down" to people who didn't have as much money. Instead of economics, critics called it Reaganomics. He won in a landslide.

Shortly after he took office, a deranged gunman tried to assassinate him outside of a hotel in Washington, D.C. While doctors got ready to take the bullet out of his lung at the hospital, he joked to Nancy, the First Lady, "Sorry, honey, I forgot to duck."

His Legacy

Reagan is remembered for pushing for the end of the Cold War with the Soviet Union (even though he once called it the "evil empire"), cutting taxes, and trying to make the government work better. "I have wondered at times," he said, "what the Ten Commandments would have looked like if Moses had run them through the U.S. Congress."

PRESIDENTIAL FIRST

Ronald Reagan was the first (and only) president to have been divorced. He was divorced from actress Jane Wyman, his first wife, and married to actress Nancy Davis, his second wife, when he took office.

FUN FACT

Reagan was hard of hearing, especially in his right ear. During his movie career in the 1930s, an actor fired a pistol near his head, which caused his hearing problems. He began wearing hearing aids in 1983—first in his right ear, then later in his left.

GEORGE H.W. BUSH

Poppy

"We are not the sum of our possessions."

Born
June 12, 1924
Milton, Massachusetts

Political Party
Republican

Vice President
J. Danforth ("Dan")
Quayle

First Lady
Barbara

Children
George W., Robin
(who died as a child),
John Ellis "Jeb," Neil,
Marvin, and Dorothy

Pet
Millie, a springer
spaniel

Before Politics

George Bush put off going to college and joined the military during World War II. He was the youngest pilot in the Navy and flew 58 combat missions in the Pacific. He won the Distinguished Flying Cross for bravery. He came home and graduated with honors from Yale, worked in the oil business, and then got into politics.

Training for the Presidency

By the time Ronald Reagan picked him to run as vice president, Bush had served in several top government jobs, including head of the Central Intelligence Agency, or CIA.

As vice president, he organized all branches of the military to cooperate and try to stop the flow of illegal drugs into the United States. Operation Blue Lightning, as it was called, equipped jets, speed boats, and helicopters with state-of-the-art sensors and tracking devices to snag drug smugglers as they tried to land on American shores.

From Vice President to President

In 1988, George Bush became the first vice president elected to president since Martin Van Buren in 1836.

He faced several foreign problems when he took office. He ordered troops to invade Panama to get rid of its corrupt dictator, Manuel Noriega. They captured Noriega and sent him to trial in Florida for drug trafficking.

When Iraq invaded Kuwait, Bush sent troops into the Persian Gulf to drive Iraq out of the country. He also saw the collapse of the Soviet Union, and more importantly, the end of the Cold War. Bush was popular for a while, but the sagging economy prevented him from getting re-elected.

Humor at the White House

As president, Bush showed his sense of humor. He once said, "I do not like broccoli. And I haven't liked it since I was a little kid and my mother made me eat it. And I'm president of the United States, and I'm not going to eat any more broccoli."

His wife, Barbara, became a spokesperson for reading and helped write *Millie's Book,* their dog's best-selling book about life in the White House.

FUN FACTS

George Bush played first base on the Yale University baseball team. His team got to the finals of the College World Series twice (but lost both times).

★★★

George H. W. Bush and his son George W. Bush are the second father and son to become president of the United States. John Adams and John Quincy Adams were the first.

WILLIAM J. CLINTON

Slick Willie

"There is nothing wrong with America that cannot be cured by what is right with America."

Born
August 19, 1946
Hope, Arkansas

Political Party
Democrat

Vice President
Albert Gore

First Lady
Hillary Rodham

Child
Chelsea

Pets
Socks, a cat;
Buddy, a dog

Meeting a President

When Bill Clinton was 16, he was an elected delegate to Boys Nation, a youth organization. The group gathered in Washington, D.C., where he met and shook hands with President John F. Kennedy. From then on, he said, Kennedy was his hero and role model—and he knew he would make a life in politics.

A Promising Future

A bright student, Clinton studied at Oxford University as a Rhodes scholar and graduated from Yale Law School. At the age of 32, he became the governor of Arkansas, the youngest governor in the country. He was elected president 14 years later.

Success Abroad and at Home

As president, Clinton gained respect in foreign countries, especially for helping to end conflict in central Europe. He also worked hard to make peace a reality in Northern Ireland and the Middle East.

He helped the economy at home, which was booming. He managed to expand international trade, and could brag about low inflation and low unemployment. He was the first Democratic president elected to a second term since FDR.

PRESIDENTIAL FIRST

Although Bill Clinton was the second president to be impeached, he was the first elected president to be impeached. Andrew Johnson (the first to be impeached) had not been elected; he became president when Lincoln was assassinated.

Impeachment

But Clinton had troubles, too. Congress refused to pass his huge health-care reform plan. And he became only the second president to be impeached—or put on trial—by the Senate for misbehavior in office. Still, he remained a very strong and powerful spokesman for the Democratic Party, and he left office as a very popular president.

FUN FACT

Bill Clinton played the saxophone in a jazz trio called Three Blind Mice in high school. He was offered several music scholarships to college, but chose to study politics instead.

A Different Kind of First Lady

Hillary Rodham Clinton went on to make history, becoming the first ever former First Lady to run for the U.S. Senate and win, and then run for her husband's old job—president of the United States. She served as U.S. secretary of state for President Obama.

HILLARY RODHAM CLINTON

October 26, 1947–

A New Role

Never a traditional First Lady, Hillary Rodham Clinton made Americans rethink the role of the president's spouse—as well as the role of women in politics. She was the first former First Lady to run for public office, to be elected to the U.S. Senate, and to serve in a president's cabinet (as one of his advisers).

From the Midwest to the East to the South

After growing up outside of Chicago in Park Ridge, Illinois, Hillary Rodham headed east to attend Wellesley College and Yale Law School. At Yale, she worked with an organization to help children and families—a lifelong passion—and met Bill Clinton, eventually moving to Arkansas and marrying him. She taught law, worked at a law firm, and become First Lady of Arkansas when her husband was elected governor.

Work, Family, and Service

Hillary Rodham (who took her husband's last name after he lost his second term as governor, thinking it would help him politically) served as First Lady of Arkansas for 12 years, balancing work, family—her daughter Chelsea was born in 1980—and public service. When Bill Clinton became president, Hillary Clinton became a new kind of First Lady. She kept an office in the West Wing of the White House, where the president's advisers had offices, and led a committee on national health-care reform, coming up with a plan designed to provide affordable health insurance for all Americans (which Congress did not pass).

A Second Act

Hillary Clinton did not retire from politics when she left the White House. She became the first woman to represent New York in the U.S. Senate, ran for the Democratic presidential nomination (winning more primaries than any other female candidate in American history), and served as secretary of state for President Obama. From first lady to secretary of state, Hillary Clinton helped redefine the role of women in politics.

FUN FACT

As a child, Hillary Clinton wrote a letter to NASA asking how to become an astronaut. NASA responded that girls could not be astronauts.

GEORGE W. BUSH
W (Dubya)

"America will never seek a permission slip to defend the security of our people."

Born
July 6, 1946
New Haven,
Connecticut

Political Party
Republican

Vice President
Richard Cheney

First Lady
Laura

Children
Barbara and
Jenna (twins)

Pets
Miss Beazley
and Barney,
Scottish terriers;
India, a cat

A Close Election

The 2000 presidential election was such a close race that it took 40 extra days to count all the votes. Finally, the Supreme Court had to decide which of the candidates—Al Gore or George W. Bush—had actually won. Even though Gore won the popular vote by a narrow margin, the high court voted 5-to-4 that Bush was the winner.

Early Days

Born in Connecticut, Bush moved as a toddler to Texas with his family and had a happy childhood.

George W. went to Yale University and then Harvard Business School, after spending a year flying F-102 fighter jets for the Air National Guard.

Terror Strikes

The governor of Texas, Bush was also, for a while, part owner of the Texas Rangers baseball team. He came to the White House wanting to improve education and lower taxes, but history stepped in and shifted his focus.

On September 11, 2001, terrorists hijacked four American airplanes and crashed two of them into the World Trade Center in New York City, one into the Pentagon (the nation's military headquarters) near Washington, D.C., and one into a field in Pennsylvania (although the plane was likely headed to the capital).

A Strong Response

President Bush declared war on terrorism. He created a new Department of Homeland Security to help make sure attacks like that wouldn't happen again. And he sent American troops to invade Afghanistan, where the terrorists had their training camps and where Osama bin Laden, the leader of the terrorists, was thought to be hiding.

Bush also became convinced that Iraq's brutal dictator, Saddam Hussein, was involved in terrorism and was hiding weapons of mass destruction (even though inspectors from the United Nations couldn't find them). He convinced Congress to authorize an invasion of Iraq, a decision that later became controversial at home and abroad.

A Tough Second Term

Bush had been a popular president during his first term, but his decision to invade Iraq, his slow response to helping people affected by Hurricane Katrina in New Orleans in 2005, and a slowdown in the U.S. economy made him less popular by the time he left office.

131

THE ROAD TO THE WHITE HOUSE

Let's say you want to be president. Are you qualified for the job? According to the U.S. Constitution, you have to be able to say yes to these three questions:

- Are you at least 35 years old?
- Are you a native-born citizen of the United States? (Were you born in the U.S.?)
- Have you been living in the United States for at least 14 years?

If you can answer yes to all these questions, you can run for president!

Political Parties and Primaries

Before you can run for president, your political party has to choose you to be its candidate. State and local governments hold elections called primaries and caucuses in late winter and spring. Political parties use these elections to determine which candidate they will nominate for president later at their national convention.

Conventions

Delegates from each political party in each state officially choose their candidate at their national convention the summer before the presidential election. Each delegate votes for his or her favorite candidate. A candidate needs to get a majority of delegate votes to win the nomination. The winner—the candidate—then chooses a vice president. Together, the presidential candidate and the vice-presidential candidate form a ticket.

The Electoral College

The candidates for each party spend the rest of the summer and part of the fall trying to convince voters that they are the right person to be president. In November, people in each state vote for who they think would make the best president. Even though voters see the candidate's name on the ballot, they are not voting directly for the candidate; instead, they are voting for a group of people in their state

called electors. These electors—who form what is called the Electoral College—are supposed to vote for their state's favorite candidate. Whichever candidate wins the most votes in a particular state generally wins all of that state's electors—winner takes all!

Electors

Different states get different numbers of electors. The number of electors equals the number of senators and representatives each state has. Every state starts with two electors—since every state has two senators—and then adds more electors depending on the population of that state. For example, a state with few people like North Dakota gets three electors; a state with lots of people like California gets 55 electors. Each elector gets one vote for president and one vote for vice president. There are a total of 538 electoral votes. A candidate needs 270 electoral votes—the majority of the electoral votes—to become president.

The winning electors then gather in December at their state capitals to cast their votes for president and vice president. In early January, the Electoral College votes are counted, and the winner—whoever gets the majority of the votes—is announced. Although this is the official result of the election, everybody knows who won on election day in November by the number of electoral votes each candidate receives.

When Winners Are Losers

Surprisingly, a candidate can win the popular vote nation-wide but still lose the election (see box). How can this happen? It all goes back to the Electoral College. If a candidate

wins a lot of popular votes but only in a few states, he will lose to a candidate who wins more states—because candidates win based on the number of electoral votes they receive, not on the number of votes the voters cast for them.

This has happened four times in U.S. history. Here are the candidates who won the popular vote but lost the election:

• Andrew Jackson lost to John Quincy Adams in 1824
• Samuel Tilden lost to Rutherford B. Hayes in 1876
• Grover Cleveland lost to Benjamin Harrison in 1888
• Al Gore lost to George W. Bush in 2000

FUN FACT

If no candidate receives the 270 votes required to win, the House of Representatives decides the election. Each state gets to cast one vote. This has happened only twice: the election of 1800 and the election of 1824.

BARACK OBAMA

Barry

"In the face of impossible odds, people who love their country can change it."

Born
August 4, 1961
Honolulu, Hawaii

Political Party
Democrat

Vice President
Joseph Biden

First Lady
Michelle

Children
Malia and Sasha

Pets
Bo, a Portuguese
water dog

From Unknown to Famous

The son of a white mother from Kansas and a black father from Kenya, Barack Obama was a largely unknown politician when he gave the keynote speech at the Democratic National Convention in 2004. But once the electrifying speech was over, people across the country knew his name.

A Global Education

Born in Hawaii, Barack Obama (or Barry, as he was known as a child) moved with his mother to Indonesia when he was six years old. She woke him up at 4 o'clock every morning to learn American school skills before sending him off to his Indonesian school three hours later. When he was ten, his mother sent him back to Hawaii to live with his grandparents and study at a nearby private school.

After college, he became a community organizer in Chicago, helping poor people find jobs and improve their living conditions. He then went to Harvard Law School.

136

Political Career

After law school and a short time working in a law firm in Chicago, he ran for the U.S. House of Representatives, but lost, and later won a seat in the U.S. Senate. In 2008 he became the first mixed-race person to be elected president of the United States.

Presidential Challenges

President Obama faced two wars and a worldwide economic recession when he took office. He sent more troops to fight in the war in Afghanistan but set a date for withdrawing soldiers from the war in Iraq. He provided hundreds of millions of dollars to make the economy grow, and gave car makers big loans so they wouldn't go out of business. He also worked to expand health care for more people. In 2011, he ordered a small military team to raid the compound of Osama bin Laden, the mastermind terrorist behind the World Trade Center attacks; bin Laden was killed in the raid.

One World

The father of two daughters, Barack Obama stressed that American people are more alike than they are different. "There is not a Black America and a White America and Latino America and Asian America," he said, "there's the United States of America."

WINGS FOR THE PRESIDENT

Symbol of the President

No matter where in the world the president travels, when he flies in *any* Air Force jet, that plane is called Air Force One. But when we hear the words Air Force One, we think of one of the two specially custom-built Boeing 747s. Brightly painted with the words "United States of America," the American flag, and the Seal of the President of the United States, Air Force One is one of the most recognizable symbols of the president, not just in this country but everywhere around the world.

Best Security

Air Force One can refuel in midair, which means it can carry the president wherever he needs to travel without landing to get fuel. It carries the most up-to-date security equipment and the best computers and telephone equipment so no one can listen in on what the president is saying when he is on board. If the United States is ever under attack, Air Force One can become a flying command center for the president!

Room for All

Inside, Air Force One has plenty of room: over 4,000 square feet on three levels. That's the size of a professional basketball court! It includes a bedroom, bathroom, and office just for the president, a conference room for staff meetings, and a separate area for reporters traveling with the president. Most of the furniture on the plane was handcrafted by master carpenters. Air Force One also has quarters for the president's senior advisors, Secret Service officers, and other guests. Several cargo planes typically fly ahead of Air Force One to provide the president with services needed in remote locations.

A doctor is always on board in case of emergency, and Air Force One includes a room with all the equipment for an operation if needed. And most important, there is a big kitchen and crew that can prepare food for 100 people.

From Propeller to Jet

Beginning with President Franklin Roosevelt, Air Force One was a propeller plane, and for the next 20 years, different propeller-driven aircraft were used by the president. In 1962, President Kennedy became the first president to use a jet aircraft, a specially build Boeing 707. The Air Force One that is being used today was first delivered to President George H. W. Bush in 1990. Both of the current Air Force One planes are maintained at Andrews Air Force base in Maryland and they are due to be replaced with new planes beginning in 2017.

INDEX

Reader's Digest Books for Young Readers

I Wish I Knew That

This fun and engaging book will give young readers a jump start on everything from art, music, literature, and ancient myths to history, geography, science, and math.

STEVE MARTIN, DR. MIKE GOLDSMITH, AND MARIANNE TAYLOR
978-1-60652-340-7

i before e (except after c)
The Young Readers Edition

Full of hundreds of fascinating tidbits presented in a fun and accessible way, this lighthearted book offers kids many helpful mnemonics that make learning easy and fun.

SUSAN RANDOL • 978-1-60652-348-3

Write (Or Is That "Right"?) Every Time

Divided into bite-size chunks that include Goodness Gracious Grammar, Spelling Made Simple, and Punctuation Perfection, this book provides quick-and-easy tips and tricks to overcome every grammar challenge.

LOTTIE STRIDE • 978-1-60652-341-4

Liar! Liar! Pants on Fire!

Sometimes the truth can be so strange that it's hard to believe. With hundreds of incredible true—and false—questions, kids have a great time testing their knowledge, learning fascinating truths, and uncovering lousy lies!

JAN PAYNE • 978-1-60652-476-3